Folktales and Ghost Stories of North Carolina's Piedmont

Theresa Bane and Cynthia Moore Brown

Schiffer Publishing Ltd

4880 Lower Valley Road, Atglen, Pennsylvania 19310

Other Schiffer Books by the Author:
Haunted Historic Greensboro, 978-0-7643-3174-9, $14.99

Other Schiffer Books on Related Subjects:
Amish Folk Tales & Other Stories of the Pennsylvania's Dutch, 978-0-7643-3809-0, $16.99
North Carolina Haunts, 978-0-7643-3790-1, $19.99
Ghosts of the North Carolina Shores, 978-0-7643-3471-9, $14.99

Designed by "Sue"
Type set in !Sketchy Times/NewBskvll BT
ISBN: 978-0-7643-3745-1
Printed in the United States of America

Schiffer Books are available at special discounts for bulk purchases for sales promotions or premiums. Special editions, including personalized covers, corporate imprints, and excerpts can be created in large quantities for special needs. For more information contact the publisher:

Published by Schiffer Publishing Ltd.
4880 Lower Valley Road
Atglen, PA 19310
Phone: 610-593-1777; Fax: 610-593-2002
E-mail: Info@schifferbooks.com

For the largest selection of fine reference books on this and related subjects, please visit our website at:
www.schifferbooks.com
We are always looking for people to write books on new and related subjects. If you have an idea for a book please contact us at the above address.

This book may be purchased from the publisher. Include $5.00 for shipping. Please try your bookstore first.
You may write for a free catalog.

In Europe, Schiffer books are distributed by
Bushwood Books
6 Marksbury Ave.
Kew Gardens
Surrey TW9 4JF England
Phone: 44 (0) 20 8392 8585; Fax: 44 (0) 20 8392 9876
E-mail: info@bushwoodbooks.co.uk
Website: www.bushwoodbooks.co.uk

Dedication

To my Prince Charming:
My patient, loving husband, Fred...
He is my champion, my best friend, my muse,
my favorite storyteller, and the funniest guy I know.
Cynthia Moore Brown

To the next generation:
Aidan James, Hannah Michelle, and Emily Joan...
This book is for each of you.
QtR - Theresa Bane

Acknowledgments

Without Theresa Bane our book would have been a long, solitary work instead of an exciting, healing adventure. Thank you, Terry!

Of course I want to thank my mother and father for all their lifelong love and encouragement to be creative. Both my families — the Moores and the Browns — have been my constant source of support, fun, and stories! Thank you to my story-loving friends in the North Carolina Storytelling Guild and North Carolina StoryFest. Gratefully, I thank Linda Evans and Betty K. Phipps of the Greensboro Historical Museum, as well as Ashley Poteat of Blandwood, for many decades of support, mutual love of history's mysteries, and my telling them. Also my friends and neighbors of Summerfield who are our extended family, and to our other extended family, the "Outing Club Gang." Most of all, thank you to my many, many "listeners"!

Cynthia Moore Brown

I would like to take this opportunity to thank those people who made this book happen: My co-author, Mrs. Cynthia Moore Brown, who is the reason we have this book; Ms. Becky Carignan, the Community Relations Manager of the Barnes and Noble at the Friendly Shopping Center in Greensboro, who first introduced me to Cynthia; Amedeo Falcone, my daddy who drove me three hours in the rain to a picnic; Gina Farago, Beta Reader extraordinaire; Mr. Robert Harris, owner of Castle McCulloch, who allowed me to take pictures of his beautifully restored property; my assistant, Joy Poger, who tirelessly and without complaint allowed herself to be dragged around yet again for both picture taking and research, even if we did lose my shoes; Ms. Doris Johnson, the wonderful UNCG student-guide; The North Carolina Storytelling Guild for its generous time and assistance; Ms. Lauren Werner, Director of Marketing at Old Salem Museums and Gardens, for her time and patience; and last but not least, the good folks at Schiffer Books, especially Ms. Dinah Roseberry and Ms. Jennifer Marie Savage.

QtR – Theresa Bane

Contents

Foreword

When Cynthia asked me to write the foreword to her collection of regional folktales and ghost stories, I was very flattered. I've known Cynthia for over thirty years. We both came to storytelling early, working in libraries. I remember crossing paths with her at library workshops and conferences where storytelling was a major component. I was always drawn to her magical and animated style of storytelling — ghost stories being her forte from the very beginning. For the seventeen years that I coordinated a storytelling festival in Raleigh, she was often one of the featured tellers. Cynthia's request for me to write the foreword also gave me pause to ask myself why I felt I might have any experience and expertise in storytelling to offer comments on this collection. Let me start by just writing a little about my becoming a storyteller.

I grew up on a large dairy farm in North Carolina in the 1950s where storytelling was as commonplace and routine as the changing shifts of cows coming and going from the milking barn. Whether it was my grandmother who lived with us, or any one of the several aunts and uncles who also lived on the farm, or one of the farmhands bringing cows in from the fields or working in the milk barn — any one of them would be likely to share an impromptu story. And it happened as a normal course of the day without any formal announcement or fanfare of "…let me tell you a story." It was just a part of the daily rhythm and conversation on the farm.

The stories ran the range from short two-minute anecdotes to full-blown epic tales. They could be as pedestrian as recounting how a cousin got the tractor stuck when he was dared to drive across the creek after a big rain or as fantastic as the time a 2,000-pound bull broke loose while he was being dehorned and almost killed one of the farmhands. Sometimes the stories were told to educate, sometimes they were told to warn, and sometimes they were told for the pure entertainment and fun of it.

While often the telling of these stories was both routine and random, there were times when the occasion and setting were more apparent and formal. Whether it was early evenings after supper or Sunday afternoons on the porch, it was expected that Grandma or Daddy or an aunt or uncle would share a story. This would invariably trigger a succession of others. The progression of these stories moved from the familial to the fantastic. Much to the delight and trepidation of us children, this would lead to our favorite — the ghost stories! These eerie tales could range from brief anecdotes to ghostly legends.

The most vivid and memorable of these tales was about Miss Ella's Ghost. Well into her nineties, Miss Ella lived alone in a large two-story house with a big wraparound porch just up the road from the dairy. The story, as it was often told to us, was that years ago a neighbor friend of Miss Ella's came by for a visit. After knocking at the front door and not getting a response, she went around back and found the kitchen door open. She went inside calling Miss Ella's name and it wasn't until she made her way upstairs that she found Miss Ella lying on the floor at the front bedroom window, her hand still clutched to the lace curtains. She had been dead for several days. The story was that if you walked by her house, especially late at night, you might see Miss Ella at the front bedroom window pulling back on the lace curtains and waving for you to come and help her.

Miss Ella's house had sat empty for many years, weathered and worn. Those of us children — my brothers and sisters, cousins, and the children of farmhands — had to walk right by Miss Ella's house to get up the road to our two favorite spots: Mr. Charlie's pond for swimming and Uncle Clyde Jones's country store for buying penny candy. And while rarely — if ever — did we walk by her house at night, even in broad daylight when walking by her house we would always stick close together, keeping our eyes on that front bedroom window watching to see if Miss Ella would appear.

Just a few weeks ago I was back home and while driving past what was once rolling cow pastures, hay fields, and weathered sheds and barns, now there's an elementary school, a large housing development, and a golf course. I drove past Miss Ella's house, which is still there, remembering that story. Of course the wraparound porch has been changed to a tall two-story porch with big columns across the front, and the house is no longer weathered and worn but covered in crisp, clean aluminum siding. And I did glance just for a second to see if Miss Ella might be standing at the upstairs window. Little did I know back then, as I huddled on the floor next to my brothers and sisters and cousins listening to the story of Miss Ella's Ghost, that years later I would share that story and many others with children throughout North Carolina.

It was in the early 1970s, after literally stumbling into a temporary job with the Wake County Public Library in Raleigh, that I found myself becoming a children's librarian and spending over twenty years there before moving on to the State Library of North Carolina as the Youth Services Consultant working with public and school librarians all over the state.

During those early years at Wake County, along with my colleagues from around the state, Cynthia being one of them, I found myself on the edge of a resurgence of storytelling — particularly in libraries. Reading stories aloud to children (story time) was the stock and trade of libraries, but a trend was developing and some librarians were putting down the books and just telling the stories. There were also rumblings of something going on in Jonesboro, Tennessee, where a group of storytellers were gathering on the porch of an old hotel and in church basements telling stories. That was the birthplace of NAPPS, the National Association for the Perpetuation and Preservation of Storytelling. Today it is the National Storytelling Network with an annual festival drawing hundreds of storytellers and thousands of story listeners from all over the world, the highlight of the three-day festival being the evening ghost stories told in the park.

At about the same time Diana Young, then Youth Services Consultant at the State Library where years later I would be in the same position, began to promote storytelling and coordinated the first statewide storytelling festival held in April 1976. Children's librarians from across the state came and told stories to school groups on the grounds of the State Capitol all week long. The goal was to encourage participants to go back home to their own libraries, schools, and communities, tell stories, and start storytelling festivals — and we did!

The very next year Wake County Public Library began a small festival on the mall outside the library in downtown Raleigh. It grew and today it is one of the few festivals across the state still being held. For seventeen years I coordinated the festival before leaving Wake County; Cynthia was one of the featured tellers brought in each year. Also out of that festival came a handful of storytellers — Terry Rollins and Dianne Hackworth to name two — who began to form what is today the North Carolina Storytelling Guild. NCSG is today a statewide organization that promotes storytelling by sponsoring festivals and workshops, and offering resources and support for our own North Carolina storytellers.

Today we have a wealth of nationally and regionally recognized storytellers in our state. We have a rich tradition of folklore, from the Appalachian tales of Jack, to the Cherokee legends, to the pirate tales of the coast, but I would venture to say, as a storyteller, a story listener, and a reader of stories, one thing has been a constant: ghost stories are some of the favorites of audiences — young and old alike. Whether it's the subtle chill of goose bumps on the back of your neck from the description of the creaking door slowly opening, or the heart-grabbing gasp from that same door slamming shut, ghost stories can elicit that contradiction of giggling laughter and shouting with fear at the same time. The mystery, the unknown, the uncertainty can be both exciting and frightening. The pictures and the sounds in the listeners' minds have no limits. And when those imaginary pictures can materialize before your eyes, as from my youth walking past Miss Ella's house and looking up at that bedroom window, it makes the story that much more of a great ride!

Cynthia's collection of stories covers all the bases — especially for ghost stories — with an added bonus for those who live right here in the Piedmont region of North Carolina. They bring the cities, the small towns, and the countryside of piedmont North Carolina to life. Eerie tales from long ago or not so long ago provide a glimpse of people and places and events — some historical and some from daily life. She has retold these stories, ranging from brief anecdotes to ghostly legends, in her own magical and energetic yet informal way. From a graveyard in Jamestown, to a haunted mansion in Greensboro, to a remote mystical spot in the woods in Chatham County—the storyteller, listener, or reader is in for a treat. What makes these stories even more accessible is that you can drive by that graveyard gate in Jamestown, visit Blandwood Manor in Greensboro, or — if you dare — go to Devil's Tramping Ground in Chatham County. These are great stories for the telling or reading aloud, or if you dare, reading alone in your room late at night! If you don't get a chance to hear Cynthia tell these stories in her own words, then at least you can read them in this collection. For you teachers, these stories can educate; for parents, guardians, and caregivers, these stories can warn of the dangers and risks out there; and for you readers, they can just be good old-fashioned entertainment.

Ron I. Jones
www.rijones.com

Preface

"I feel a story coming on, be still and listen to me."

It was all the way back in 2007 when I was working on my first Schiffer book, *Haunted Historic Greensboro*, that I was introduced to my coauthor. I was driving to a convention when my cell phone rang. It was Becky Carignan, the Community Relations Manager of the Barnes and Noble at the Friendly Shopping Center in Greensboro. She knew that I had been looking for haunted historic places in the city for my book and said that she knew of someone who may be able to help me, Greensboro's very own storyteller, Cynthia Moore Brown.

About a week later my assistant, Joy (also known as "Skuttles"), and I traveled to Summerfield, a bucolic little town just a hair outside of Greensboro's city limits to Cynthia's house where we all met for the first time. I knew from that very first meeting that she and I were going to be friends. We had tea on her patio surrounded by her well-loved and tended garden, filled with sweet-smelling flowers, hummingbirds, and ladybugs. There, we talked at length about "Lydia," the phantom hitchhiker of Jamestown, as well as the ghostly goings-on at Blandwood Manor and Devil's Tramping Ground. To put it mildly, she was a wealth of information. As she told us the stories, even casually over tea, Joy and I were captivated and hanging on every word she spoke.

When her tales were told, we couldn't help ourselves — Joy and I applauded, smiling widely, like two little giggling girls. I asked Cynthia if she had a book out, as I felt like I needed to buy it and take her stories home with me to read to myself and share with others. While she warmed up my tea she went on to explain that she'd like to have a book one day, that her head was so full up with stories she'd like to get out and onto paper, but didn't know quite how to go about doing it.

Not long afterwards, our partnership was born.

For a communal point of reference, folklore, by definition, is the knowledge, songs, and stories of our beliefs and traditions. It is usually taught informally in small groups, if there is ever any training at all. Usually storytellers are those individuals who have a natural gift for telling a tale and with a bit of refinement can reach a professional level. The story itself is expressed through actions and words in a creative performance that educates and entertains. Folktales teach us not just who we are and where we came from but also how to make sense of the world we live in.

Storytelling is more than relating a tale to an audience, and folklore is more than a collection of old tales. Anyone can tell you what happened way back when, but it takes a master of the craft, a true Storyteller, to say it in such a way that you experience the drama as the tale unfolds. Part of writing this book was discovering for myself how the storyteller connects with their audience, and capturing that exchange of energy between the teller and their audience and transferring it here into the written word.

A Storyteller is someone who takes on the mantle of this time-honored tradition and is able to express themselves so that their intent is understood. They are truly able to relate their tale to their audience because they are intimately familiar with the subject matter and they can clearly see the story they are telling unfolding in their head as they speak. As they tell their tale, the story progresses, and by use of vocalization and body language they are able to infer to their audience even what they do not say with words. Sometimes to be able to do this well or believably requires a bit of research on the teller's part long before the tale is told, but usually a Storyteller is born local to their tales and it is a part of who they are, and always has been.

When Cynthia and I conspired to write this book, it was our intent that the stories would be written exactly as she told them — and that I would record and transcribe them verbatim. It was a wonderful idea in theory, if not on paper, as it did not take into account the "how" of how she told her tale. Cynthia uses more than body language when she tells her stories. She screams, she laughs, and she sobs out dialogue. Stamping her feet and clapping her hands she is also the slamming of a door or the crack of lightning. Her action words are said aloud as they are performed. She never tells her audience that the old woman is bent and frail, but rather she shows them that by doubling over, her body trembling, shuffling as she walks. When she speaks for the old woman, she never once tells them that her voice is unsteady and scratched, but rather speaks that way to them. A great deal of written words needed to be added to the story so that readers could "see" what Cynthia's audience did, but the physicality of her storytelling is only just part of it.

For instance, when she says that a tree is tall and has long branches that look like skeletal fingers, naturally her voice takes on an ominous and drawn-out, deep tone. However, what the tape recorder cannot capture is that she is also slowly stretching out her arms toward her audience, standing on her tiptoes, leaning over the listeners in the first row and using her own hands and fingers to emphasize the tree branches. I found that I had to take written notes to accompany my tapes for later transcriptions. It was essential to capture not only Cynthia's voice when creating the stories for a book, but also the mood she sets as well.

Mrs. Cynthia Moore Brown, dressed in her Halloween finest, is ready to perform in the graveyard near Blandwood Manor, Greensboro, North Carolina.

These gestures and the obvious vocal emphasis she utilizes during her telling are called "markers," and they not only help her tell her tales, but they are also an imbedded part of her storytelling. This happens so naturally for her that she is perhaps even unaware as she unconsciously feeds off her audience's emotions, gauging their reactions to her actions and playing off them. The more scared her audience looks, the scarier she becomes. When it's time for her to stomp a foot, clap her hands, and holler out "BOO!", every person out there jumps in their seat, letting out first a small squeal, followed by a little nervous laughter. She always pauses just long enough for her audience to collect themselves and come back to the story with her, usually by saying something like "And dontcha know what happened next?"

On the other hand, in her seasonal role as Mrs. Claus, Cynthia dons a red velvet gown decked out with white fur trim, gold-rimmed

Cynthia in her role of Mrs. Clause. Parents who remember Cynthia telling them stories when they were young are now enjoying taking their own children to see their favorite storyteller. *Photo by Theresa Bane*.

glasses, and black boots. In no way does she resemble the black-clad, witchy storyteller of the fall season, but rather a warm and grandmotherly figure. At events, she does not merely step onto a stage, but rather walks in the room, thanking the elves over her shoulder for dropping her off and hollering out a gentle reminder to them not to forget to come back in an hour or so to pick her up. At that time she walks through the room, in one hand jingling a strap of bells as she waves and sends out a warm welcome to everyone who came to hear her, making eye contact and giving out the occasional little wink. Hanging off one elbow is a basket filled with candy canes. The other has her appropriately seasonal purse with a few of her props sticking out — an antique doll for telling her version of Little Red Riding Hood and an electric harp. Cynthia has it all, her voice, gestures, expressions, dress, and stage presence all come together to have every child present, and maybe a few adults too, drawn in, really and truly believing that she is Mrs. Claus. Not because she is an actress plying a trade, but this too is part of the storytelling, weaving visually so that later as she speaks it will help her listeners visualize the story she tells from the heart. She tells the tale but your mind fills in the scenery all around her.

As you can see, when it came time to sit down and write out her stories I wasn't merely having to transcribe her words but also having to invest the story with her energy. In order to capture the mood that she creates with voice and motion, I had to use a lot of words to compensate. Sometimes I found that there was a one to seven ratio, especially in the longer stories. To add to this, I had to do so in such a way that it maintained her "voice." This was not such an easy task, as the vernacular for dialogue was particularly difficult, but I feel that you will find the results pleasing.

Although numerous folktale books are already on the market, this book has a unique claim. Not only does it have for the first time anywhere the stories of Cynthia Moore Brown in print, but also four new tales created just for this project: "The Hunter of Purgatory Mountain," "The Gold in the Lake," "The Spirits of Abbotts Creek," and my personal favorite, "The Hero, Valentine Leonard." Each one of these stories were newly researched and added to Cynthia's ever-increasing arsenal of folklore. There may come a day when you hear those tales told by others but when you do just remember that it was Cynthia who first pulled them together and shared them with the world. Although it is true, the story of Lydia, the Phantom Hitchhiker of Jamestown, is well known through the area and many books tell her story, none of them have Cynthia's unique rendition.

The stories have been grouped by areas rather than presented strictly alphabetically. This was done because I have found that for those individuals, historians, and folklorists alike who research the lore of a given area, they prefer to know beforehand exactly where a certain story is said to have taken place.

Among the resources I utilized — books, articles, and personal interviews of paramount importance was the North Carolina Storytelling Guild (NCSG). It was an invaluable resource to me. Its members are a close-knit, friendly group and more than welcoming to anyone who loves a good story. I am sure that whether you are just starting out in the field of storytelling or a seasoned veteran, you will find that you agree. If you cannot make it to one of their events, their website, www. ncstoryguild.org, is full of helpful articles and links.

Whether you've heard the story before or not, I invite you to go to the area it takes place in and see for yourself the land there, make a connection with the past, and share it with others.

Introduction

Mysteries and folktales, especially the unsolved kind, are audience and reader favorites. Everyone loves a good mystery! Old and young, girls and guys alike, there seems to be no one group that craves them more than another. Everybody loves a good story, especially when it's told in a compelling way. Mysteries and folktales are my favorite to tell, to read, and to write. They're also my most requested when I perform for storytelling programs and concerts.

Now of course the telling of folktales transcends human history. For thousands of years, even before the written word, the storytellers were chronicles of civilization's history. Every culture throughout the ages has had its storytellers. Not just for entertainment purposes either. No, instead they were an essential element of the people. Folktales bring history and its mysteries to life for the listeners.

Cynthia performs in front of a live audience at Stedman Elementary School, Stedman, North Carolina, April 2010. *Photo by Fred Brown.*

I have performed and told stories, folktales, and mysteries for most all of my life and have done so professionally since 1974. I began as a librarian using my beloved picture books for the outreach program that Joe Ferguson and I took to places like preschools, daycare homes, and Head Start. They loved the books and so did we, yet, when you put the book down to show later and instead just tell the story, the audience responds in a far different way. The storytelling also made possible large audiences.

I have been frequently asked where my ideas for stories begin. Sometimes I hear an anecdote, joke, or folktale and then adapt it. Other times I find something intriguing or mysterious about a person, place, or structure and I "write" a story for it using my imagination. For instance, some examples include…when I lived in the haunted log cabin on Horse Pen Creek Road, or the incidents of ghostly noises and handprints I was told about when I went to afternoon tea at Wisteria Cottage. It's been amazing to me the wealth of stories you can find if you open your mind to the possibilities. All these years I told the story, then retold it, retold it, and retold it until I had it crafted out perfectly. Yet, I had always skipped the important step of putting the words to the story down on paper. Rather, I have stored thousands and thousands of words in my memory to retell the stories. Oh, I have a list of my titles. I did write out the ones I told on my CD "Ghost Stories From the Graveyard," but that is only because I had to do it. According to Tom, the sound engineer at Sound Lab, he and I had to have a point of reference while laying down the tracks for each story. Tom had me in the sound booth (really a closet!) telling my stories as if I were in front of two hundred eager listeners. That was really a fun time; I felt like a rock star!

However, the majority of my favorites I continue to retell. I "write" orally a story about a place or occurrence so I then remember it vividly. During a session at a North Carolina Storytelling Guild Winter Workshop there was a heated discussion about this very method. Some of the participants had not written any adaptations on paper, while others, like Kelly Swanson, write all theirs before telling them the first time.

That's why it was so exciting to meet and connect with Terry — it was incredible to share each word of my orally written stories with her after which I could then see the completed written story she penned. She captured my "voice," the way I phrase and execute the words, when she wrote down my story. She is so talented. She was able to capture the essence of the story even before we knew each other very well. Another advantage to having the story in the written word is that we have is that they are here for you and many others to read and experience regardless of their audience membership whoever, whenever. So now, thanks to Terry, I can be sure my stories are saved in print as well as the oral tradition.

I first began to write the mysteries of history on my mother's old typewriter. I began when I was only eleven or twelve years old. Oddly enough, I was not yet telling stories. I kept the folder and to this day I tell some of them: the haunted mansion on the hill, baby-sitting at the funeral home next door, or finding the old gravestones in our forest explorations in our backyard.

Why are folktales and mysteries the genre I prefer? Well... I grew up in a family of good storytellers, history buffs, and humorists. My father had traveled the world with the U.S. Navy. He came home to tell the tales of magical worlds of the ancients as well as telling us about the art, culture, and mysteries of Europe's present. My dad's family, the Moores, lived in a 100-year-old creaky house in a small Ohio town. When we visited in the summers, Grandma Moore would tell us the adventures of "Little Orphan Annie" and other tales as well. She and my grandfather, along with my many great-aunts, enjoyed bringing our long family history to life. Nowadays my dear, dear mother, Miriam, who still has her spirit and fire at eighty-plus years old, regales us with tales of her life, love, and adventures growing up in a far different era. I believe we should honor our elders by recording their stories, listening, and encouraging the oral tradition. Their link with the past is invaluable. It is so important to preserve their stories.

Cynthia during a performance at Northwoods Elementary School in February 2010. *Photo by Brooke Taylor, Northwoods Elementary School.*

Cynthia during a performance at the Grand Bohemian Hotel ballroom, Asheville, North Carolina, July 2010. *Photo by Frankie Olmsted.*

When I was eleven, we moved to a house that was said not only to be more than 200 years old, but haunted as well. It was located on a quiet street in Wickford, a small village on Narragansett Bay in Rhode Island. This was the perfect place for a wild, creative imagination to blossom. I loved it there! This old home place with decades of people and their histories was full of opportunities. There was even a haunted old mansion on the hill near our home. We kids weren't supposed to go over there because of the dangers, but of course we didn't listen — we had to explore. All this potential knowledge just added to my already extreme interest. So it's no wonder that I invented all kinds of stories and scenarios that played out in my mind. Our old haunted house was especially good for inspiration with all its creaks and groans, the doors that swung open, and the stairway to the very spooky attic, but, spooky or not, that attic was where I loved to spend sunny and rainy afternoons alike. That is, when my brother Mack and I were not spending some free time of our daylight hours exploring and playing in the old forest that sprawled out behind our house.

I grew up in the 1950s and 1960s, and it was quite a different world back then from the world we live in today — safer, slower, more caring people, especially in that quiet old village that we lived in. There were no twenty-four-hour-a-day news channels blaring of war, murder, and mayhem. Back then, we Wickford teenagers loved "slumber parties" (sleepovers is what you call 'em now). Ours were candle-lit, of course, and filled with my stories, Ouija boards, and fake séances. I didn't know then just how important the stories of people were. We just knew that we liked hearing them and telling them. Thankfully, some of the really important things haven't been lost through the years.

So that's it — the whole beginning and middle part of the story. Now you're going to have the thrill of "the end."

I hope you enjoy the stories we chose. Most of them are my longtime favorites but there are a few that we wrote and created just for this book. They are waiting to be told aloud. I, of course, love the stories of Summerfield and just had to give them to you. When we began working, I did more extensive research on some of the stories. Once I got involved, there were countless characters reaching out. I wrote my "author notes" to them so you'd feel a link to how I encountered some of the people, places, and spirits. The intriguing historical facts involving Valentine Leonard and my husband's family ancestors were too compelling to ignore. Valentine spoke to me as they say, "from the grave" with his incredible life and heroic death. This is a perfect example of the power of stories. They have the power to be strong enough to persevere over time. For over 250 years they have been told and cherished by the living. That's the heart-to-heart of folklore. If you can, visit Pilgrim Church and its unique ancient graveyard in Lexington, North Carolina. Standing there amongst all those long-dead families and war heroes, I felt them pulling me closer to see just a glimpse of what had been.

So yeah! Here are a few of my stories for you to experience. We are giving you the stories to read as I would tell them; it's almost as if you and I were having our own candlelit storytelling adventure. Light a fire, make some comfy tea or hot cocoa, and as you read, imagine I am telling you the story.

Cynthia Moore Brown
Summerfield, North Carolina
March 11, 2010

Chapter One:
Asheboro
Home of North Carolina's Zoo

The town of Asheborough, as it was originally spelled when it was granted its charter on Christmas Day 1796, was named for Governor Samuel Ashe. Citizens of Randolph County had demanded that the county seat be relocated to a more centralized area and, upon a fifty-acre tract of land, the county courthouse was built on Asheborough's Main Street Square. Not so long after that a two-story courthouse was built followed quickly by several law offices. For over on hundred years court related business was the business of Asheborough, North Carolina.

In 1829, the town formalized its government and reincorporated so that improvements could be made. It had, by this point, an official post office, a weekly newspaper, *The Southern Citizen*, and nearly one hundred citizens. Money from the nearby gold mills, such as Castle McCulloch, was finding its way into town.

The Civil War came and went, and Asheborough itself changed very little until the Southern Railroad arrived in 1889. A bank and the Southern Telephone Company soon followed, and the population began to double every year. Manpower and money led to the opening of a number of factories, a foundry, as well as lumber and textile mills. A railroad accident followed by a sweeping fire necessitated that the center of town be relocated to Sunset Avenue and a new courthouse was built there. Electricity and a well-fed water supply started to become standard just as the fire department, a public school, and hospital were established.

In 1923, for no reason that anyone has been able to discover, the United States Post Office took it upon itself to change the name of "Asheborough" to "Ashboro," but folks wouldn't have it. After numerous protests and complaints, a compromise was reached and the town was officially named "Asheboro."

Business slowed during the Great Depression here like it did most everywhere else, but after World War Two there was a sudden boom in construction and the openings of industrial plants, many of which are still here and in operation today, such as B. B. Walker Shoe Company, Black and Decker, Eveready Battery Company, Georgia Pacific, and Klaussner Furniture Industries.

Today the city of Asheboro has nearly 25,000 residents. It also has the bragging rights to being the home of the North Carolina Zoological Park and Gardens, the world's largest natural habitat zoo with 500 acres.

The Hunter of Purgatory Mountain

Watercolor by Cynthia.

It happens mostly on the darkest of nights. You can see a figure up there on the ridge or on the top of a hill. Sometimes you can see it at dusk just as the sun is setting. It's especially visible in the fall on foggy nights. What it is that folks claim to see? It's the figure of a man. This figure of a man, as he stands there with his long coat flapping open in the breeze, looks down on you as if passing some sort of judgment upon you as he wanders along the cliff edge. There are times when his spirit is so faint that you can hardly see anything of him at all. There are long stretches of time when no one sees him and people begin to think that he's finally gone, but he's not gone. He's never leaving. Folks don't talk about him much, but everyone knows who it is — the Hunter of Purgatory Mountain.

In truth, most folks don't like to call the mountain by its real name; rather, they call it the Uwharrie Mountains, but that's not wholly true.

Back during the Civil War, many men and young teenaged boys were taken into service by the army down in what's now known as Asheboro and Seagrove, in the area where the wonderful North Carolina Zoo was built. That whole area remains mysterious. The part that they call the Uwharrie Mountains is not a mountain like the Alps are mountains, not even a mountain like the Appalachians are mountains. The Uwharrie Mountains are old, old, old and really now are a lot more like a great big hill.

No matter what you call it, the whole area for centuries now has been very historic. Potters and artists from England and Germany came to North Carolina and located there because the earth was so rich and special, and it was especially excellent for making pottery, which they became famous for. Their trade and skill was made into a tradition passed down from father to son and mother to daughter — and this great folk tradition continues on to this very day. You can go on down there and visit Seagrove — what folks say is the foot of the Uwharrie Mountains — and you can actually see the pottery and the glazes that were first perfected hundreds of years ago.

Still this place remains mysterious…

During the Civil War there was a settlement of Quakers that lived in that area, at the foot of Purgatory Mountain as well as in the valley it formed. Because it was a time of war, many of the men of the community had already gone off to fight. Everyone was so desperate for the war to end, especially toward the end when there was hardly enough men left to fight in the last few battles. The army sent a recruiter man here and he became known as the Hunter.

The Hunter rode in, tall and overbearing. When the mothers saw him riding into town, they closed up their shutters and locked their children up inside, from the teenage boys to their very youngest. The Hunter was coming to take whichever of the boys he could catch because the war effort was that desperate. And that's just what the evil, bad man did. He went from door to door, house to house, and forced the families to let him take their teenage boys away. He even forced them to let him take their younger boys, the ones who were only eleven or twelve years old, an age that is far too young to go off fighting in a war.

When the Hunter had a nice small group of them, because that was really all that was left in the town by then, he marched them away from their family and friends, out of the community. He planned to march them all the way out to the coastal town of Wilmington. There he intended to assemble them and make them ready to fight in a war, but these boys were smart boys — and clever too. Along the way, in the dead of night, in the cold of winter, as they sat close together, shivering and hungry, cold and wanting nothing more than to be back home by the fire, they came up with a plan to escape. When night fell and was at its darkest, late, late in the evening, the Hunter himself lay sleeping in a dreamless, dead sleep, the sleep brought on by the exhaustion that evil brings. That was when the boys were able to slip away.

The oldest ones helped the younger ones and the younger ones helped each other. They had to be careful as they moved in the dark of night. It was cold and frigid and snowy and icy, as North Carolina was a much colder place back then. They knew that if they so much as fell for one moment into one of the rain-swollen or snow-swollen rivers that they would die, but they made it. The boys made it all the way back to the center of the state, back to the Uwharrie Mountains…Purgatory Mountain.

At first they had to hide in the woods during the day. At night they would take turns sneaking back to their homes in small groups to visit their beloved families. Their mothers were so thrilled to have them back home, even for a little while. The boys were fed some good and nutritious food while they sat by the home fire, but always before dawn came, the boys had to slip back, unseen, into the woods, slip back into hiding. They had to because of the Hunter.

The Hunter… The Hunter was said to have been so furious to have failed in his mission that he mounted up on his horse and came racing up a storm back to the community. He arrived not too long after the boys had arrived. For safety the boys had gone deep into hiding, but the Hunter didn't know that — and he didn't care. He burst into the home of Mrs. Smith, the mother of one of the boys he had taken, and demanded the child back.

The mother, Mrs. Smith, could honestly say to the Hunter, "Well, I have no earthly idea where my son Tyler is — look around for yourself. It's just the baby and little Sally and me."

The Hunter was furious. He went from house to house and it seemed like his rage just grew and grew until it made him crazy. Making matters worse, he imagined that his superiors were laughing at him — they had to be. They were laughing at him all over the state. What kind of recruiter was he that a bunch of little boys got away?

He paced back and forth, back and forth in the house he lived in. Every night he paced relentlessly in front of the fire.

The boys always kept an eye on his house. Whenever any of them would slip away home for a visit, they had to stay a shorter and shorter length of time because they were so afraid that at any moment the Hunter would burst into their mother's home and grab them. The only thing they could do was to make the Hunter leave.

As spring came, the weather warmed up a little bit and life was a little easier on the boys, but the Hunter was still just about crazy with fury. He would go out up on the ridge of Purgatory Mountain and look down at the community below. There he would rant and rave to nobody about nothing as he paced back and forth, stomping with anger as he went. "Where are those boys?" he wondered. "If we lose the war, it will be all my fault!"

By now the Hunter was completely out of his mind and the boys realized that he was not going to leave, maybe not ever. The war was all but over anyway and still he was there, trying to catch them, storming through the woods, looking for them as he went. Luckily, the boys were always too clever for the Hunter and he never did grab any of them.

Three of the oldest boys got to talking one night as they sat around their small fire in the deep, deep valley in the woods. They were the best marksmen in the group and they decided that something had to be done. "We can't keep letting that Hunter terrorize us and our families. Some of our fathers are not coming home and we are the men now. There is only one thing we can do to get rid of him."

So one morning the three eldest boys got up very early, long before any of the other boys. Without telling a soul, the three of them went out with the one lone gun they had and with it they waited at the edge of the woods.

It was the custom of the Hunter to come out of his cabin in the morning and go into the community to demand breakfast from one family or another. On this morning, however, it was a little bit warmer than usual and the Hunter took a moment to walk over to the edge of the mountain and look down on the community below. He looked as if he had spotted something interesting, maybe a shadow he suspected to be hiding the boys. Then, out of the predawn darkness — POW! A single gunshot rang out. Just one. The Hunter, the evil terror of Purgatory Mountain, fell.

Three of the younger boys crept out of their hiding place and looked all around. No one else was there. No one had heard the shot yet; no one was running their way. The three older boys crept over to the Hunter and saw that he was indeed dead, but just telling the others would not be enough. To prove it to them they cut the buttons off his uniform coat and then vanished back into the woods.

Time went by. Some of the soldiers came back from the war. The stories were told about how terrible life had been for the families that had been harassed by the Hunter. The boys who had been taken by him had all gone back to their homes. They grew up into fine men. Life continued back on Purgatory Mountain and in the valley below. The Hunter was never seen or heard from again.

Then, one day, a couple of years later, Mary and her sweetheart, John, had stayed out too late. They had been picking blackberries and walking around the base of the mountain when Mary stopped and suddenly said, "Look! Look! There is someone on the cliff."

John looked to where Mary was pointing and indeed there was someone. It seemed to be a man just standing there on the edge of the mountain, his coat blowing open in the wind, but then a moment later… the figure was suddenly gone. It was as if the person had just jumped off the cliff. John and Mary ran to where they thought the man would have fallen to, but there was no one there and neither of them had ever heard him so much as cry out for help.

After they told their story, more and more people began to see a figure of a man, especially at dusk, standing up there on the ridge of the mountain. Why, if you look up there, every once in a while you can see a man, tall and pale, standing there, his coat blowing in the wind, even when there isn't any wind blowing. Sometimes he was seen pacing back and forth along the edge. It didn't take long for the story to start up again that the Hunter of Purgatory Mountain had returned. They said it was because his spirit could not rest in peace so it had to walk back and forth, back and forth along that ridge for all time.

About Seagrove

I began going down to Seagrove in the early 1970s to learn pottery and buy the beautiful bowls, cups, and plates at Cole's Pottery. Each handmade piece was just a few dollars. They opened the kiln early Saturday mornings, setting their pottery on sawhorse tables in the shed near the old chicken coop that was now the pottery throwing area. Inside were all the pottery wheels where you could watch Nell Cole and her family make the pieces. Their glazes, shapes, and traditions have been passed down, along with their stories, for many generations and continue to this day. All these years later we still use my favorite cobalt blue dishes.

The Gentleman Ghost of Uwharrie Mountain

Many years ago, there was a long and winding path that traveled through the Uwharrie Mountains and led from Greensboro to Asheboro. The path was there before the founding of either town. These days, you would just take Highway 220 and get there in no time, but in the time before there was a highway, people did not travel from city to city, but rather from town to town, and if you wanted to get to Asheboro, the only reasonable way to do so was to take that path through the mountains, but never at night. Not even the Indians who first settled in the area would travel the mountain path at night.

Geologically speaking, the Uwharrie Mountains are not technically mountains at all, just very large hills. Nevertheless, they have always kept that Indian name just as it has always been a treacherous undertaking to journey down the path at night. There have always been stories about strange goings-on in those hills. Some folks believed there was a mysterious force that caused it; others claimed it was ancient magic. Although no one knew for certain what the source of the trouble was, they did know one thing for certain: it was strongest and most active at night.

Tom and Addie Mae had not been married for very long. Although the happy event took place in Greensboro, Tom's family lived in Asheboro. Since they had missed the celebration of the nuptials, the newlyweds

This private residence in Onslow County, North Carolina, is an example of the mansions of by-gone eras. *Photo by Cynthia*.

decided that a trip over the mountain was in order. A few days later, the young couple rose before the dawn, hitched up Tom's horses to the wagon, and began the lengthy ride to and through the Uwharrie Mountains.

It was a tedious ride, longer than their youthful enthusiasm had anticipated, for as the day wore on, they did not make very good time. The shadows grew longer and longer, and soon it became dark. Not wanting to stop just yet, believing they could still make the journey in one day, they decided to press on. The temperature began to drop, and then as often happens on the mountain, a fog began to roll in and gather. Soon, they were traveling in near total darkness.

Addie Mae, new bride that she was, became more and more annoyed as they traveled further on into the night. She fixated on the cold and the dark until she was so perturbed about the situation she was unable to keep quiet about it any longer.

"Tom, I just cannot understand why we cannot go any faster," the words bursted suddenly out. "I am tired, I want to go to bed, and I want to go to sleep." Before Tom could reply, she continued on. "And I am hungry. All I can think about is that you promised me one of your mama's home-cooked meals tonight." She let out a long and forlorn sigh, wrapping her homespun blanket tightly around her shoulders. "I reckon we ain't gonna make it. We're just gonna hafta find an inn or at the very least somebody's nice house to stay in, you know."

Now you have to remember, this was back in the days when there were no highways, no rest stops, and no hotels. Yet, folks still needed a place to spend the night when they traveled. Fortunately, those were gentler days and it was the custom back then that when it grew dark, a weary traveler could knock upon the door of a stranger and expect his hospitality. The host would offer to put the traveler up for the night, typically giving him permission to sleep in the barn, but every so often, the host would have an extra room in his house and would offer that instead.

Tom, trying to get his marriage off to a good start, agreed with his new bride and they began to strain their eyes looking out into the dark for even a hint of light that would indicate they were near someone's home. As they continued along the centuries-old path, they saw nothing. In fact, it was becoming doubly heart-wrenching because it also felt as if they were getting no closer to the town of Asheboro as well. With a deep sigh and a heavy heart, Tom finally admitted sheepishly to his lovely Addie Mae, "I'm sorry, but I reckon we're just gonna hafta stop for the night and maybe sleep under the wagon."

Addie Mae grabbed Tom by the arm and she pointed out across his chest into the darkness. "Tom!" she yelled excitedly. "Stop the wagon, stop! Look, gates! Gates and a driveway!"

A Safe Haven?

Tom strained his eyes and looked down Addie Mae's arm. There it was, just barely visible in the darkness, two overly large and ornate wrought iron gates. They stood open and appeared to be welcoming them to turn their wagon onto its long and winding drive.

The couple turned their horses off the well-worn path and onto the drive beyond the gates. They huddled closer together, for as they followed their new path, the fog grew thicker and higher. The tall trees that lined either side of the road seemed to be leaning in over them, their empty branches reaching out like long, skeletal fingers.

Addie Mae kept tight-lipped, a shiver running through her. She pulled her blanket closer around her shoulders and regretted seeing the gates. Just as she was about to turn to Tom and beg him to circle the wagon around back to the road, they came to the end of the driveway and there before them stood a huge and stately mansion. It was tall and imposing with several floors, designed more like the grand mansions of the past, with gables, towers, archways, and a widow's walk. There was also a gatehouse that they could see, as well as various other outbuildings, including a large barn.

Do these gates lead to a place of refuge for a travel-weary couple? Or is something more sinister awaiting them? *Illustration by T. Glenn Bane.*

All previous reservations, fears, and concerns simply melted away from Addie Mae when she had finally taken in the whole view. Starry-eyed and filled with amazement, she mused, "Why, this place will surely have some nice folks. They must have some extra rooms in there." As soon as the notion of spending a night in that house occurred to her, she began to wonder what the room and the bed would look like. "Oh, come on, Tom, let's go on up there and get out of this wagon, quick!"

Tom hurried his team of horses up to the house. He noted that whoever the master of this house was, he had to be a wealthy man indeed, as every window in the huge mansion was brightly shining out into the night.

The couple walked hand-in-hand up the few marble steps that were lined with lanterns to a set of grand, yet thick wooden doors. The doors were also lantern lit, and their light shone brightly off the set of ornately carved brass door knockers.

Tom grabbed one of the knockers, his fingers barely making it all the way around the thick metal circle, and he let the weight of it fall loudly several times against the doors. Shockingly, although the knocker was solid brass and the doors obviously solid and thick, the sound that rang out was hollow. It painfully reverberated throughout the inside of the home, echoing down every hall and passageway.

Several long and quiet moments passed. They both stood on that brightly lit marble porch and waited for any sign or indication that someone was coming to open the door. There would have been no missing the noise the knocker had made, and yet, no one ever answered the door.

Addie Mae was shivering with cold; her blanket was about useless against it. She was thinking hard about what the room would look like that would be offered them for the night. She implored Tom to try knocking again, harder this time. He lifted the brass ring and, putting just a little effort into it, made an even more monstrous noise that rang out, cutting into the night, frightening the horses. The sound echoed throughout the house for a long while, and yet, still no one came to answer the door.

It was obvious that there could not be a living soul inside that house. Addie Mae was growing colder, if that were at all possible at this point. She turned to Tom and began to make an argument that they should just go ahead and sleep in the barn anyway, figuring that in the morning when the people who lived here made themselves apparent, they could explain... The rest of what she had to say was cut off by a hair-curling screech. Snapping their heads to the side, the couple turned to see that the door, thick and heavy, was slowly creaking open.

No one was there. They had full well expected to see a manservant or even a maid standing there, but they were not at all prepared to see no one.

Beyond the place where someone should have been standing they saw a long and empty, but brightly lit, hallway. Just off to the right was a lavish and beautifully furnished parlor. The rugs on the floor were brightly colored and thick and lush. Fancy solid silver candelabras were throughout. There was a massive stone fireplace with a roaring fire. Flanking it on either side were a set of tall and overstuffed wing back chairs.

Addie Mae was so excited that before she could even think to stop herself, she walked right on in and straight to one of the wingback chairs. As soon as she sat down, she kicked off her boots and warmed her feet at the fire. Her own blanket, thin and worn, was left on the floor beside her. She discovered one next to her on the chair, new and clean smelling, and heavier than any she had ever owned. It took no time at all for her to warm right up and begin to allow herself to get drowsy.

Tom waited until she had settled down into the chair and had tucked herself under the blanket. He waited a moment, but that was all it took before she was fast asleep. Figuring that she would be safe there, he decided to look around a little, as they still did not have permission to be inside the house.

The downstairs of the mansion was huge and it took him a long while to look into each room. Still, he was able to find no one. There was a flight of overly wide and winding stairs that led to the next level, and he was tempted to take them, but decided against it. He didn't want to abuse the rules of hospitality and invade anyone's privacy, so he called up the stairs.

His "hello" echoed throughout the mansion, bouncing off every surface and taking a long time to fade off into nothing. Tom looked around while he waited for a response. The walls were covered with intricate and expensive tapestries — except in one place. There hung a wooden plaque and what should have held a pair of crossed swords, held only one.

Uncomfortable with exploring the house any further, Tom felt he could look around outside more freely. He went back down the long hall and to the parlor they had first come upon. Addie Mae was now snug and deeply asleep. Tom went and made sure his new bride was tightly tucked into the chair, kissed her forehead, and quietly slipped out of the room, trying very hard not to let his old boots make too much noise on the floor.

Tom checked on his team of horses and then went walking off onto the grounds. It had occurred to him that perhaps the master of the house and his entire staff was out here somewhere for some reason. It would have to be a good reason; after all, it was cold and there was a thick fog that persisted even in the now-falling rain and no one would light every candle in the house, build up a roaring fire, and then leave unless something very important had happened.

Addie Mae stirred a bit in the chair, drifting in the place between sleep and waking. She was just lapsing back into slumber when she recognized what that sound was. It must have woken her up, the sound of the heavy footfall of boots on the floor. "Oh, that must be Tom. He has big old boots." Figuring that her new husband had been successful in his search for the master of the house, she stretched out and peeked around the corner of the chair, looking down. She wanted to see if he was tracking dirt through this nice home.

Instead, she saw the nicest pair of boots she'd ever seen. They were of hard leather, black, and polished to a shine. She knew right away that could not be her Tom, but rather the owner of the house. Figuring that she was now the person to make first contact with the owner, she quickly began speaking so as not to be thought of as a robber.

"Well, hello," her excited and rambling outburst began. "I am ever so sorry we came right in like this, but we did knock and the door just opened on up. My name is Addie Mae, and my husband's outside looking for you, I imagine. Oh, but you'll love him like I do. His name is Tom, and he is just so sweet."

From his boots, she began to look up at him. He wore trousers of fine material, a ruffled shirt like the old-time lords and gentlemen used to wear, and over that was a fancy cutaway waistcoat.

She was still talking, but over the sound of her own voice, she heard him speak. "Good evening." The voice was a genuinely deep baritone, cultured and proper sounding.

She had finally managed to get the heavy blanket off herself and stand up from the wing back chair. She stepped out from around it, smiling, wanting to make a good first impression on the man in the expensive suit.

She had imagined him to be handsome from the sound of his voice, with a chiseled face and classical good looks. At first she thought her eyes were playing a trick on her, and then she thought herself to still be asleep and dreaming it, but the heat from the fireplace now to her back was real enough, so it had to be true. Her scream was choked back because the man who stood before her had no head. Yes, there atop his elegant and well-built shoulders was ... *no* head and *no* face.

Speak No Evil

Eventually the scream came, and she thought it would never stop. The air finally gone from her lungs triggered her body into action. Her legs began to walk her back out of the room and she gasped for air several times, preparing herself to run.

"Please," he took a step cautiously in her direction, his arm reaching out to her with his perfectly manicured fingers not fully extended, as if he were holding onto some last bit of hope. "Don't leave. Don't be afraid. I've been waiting here for someone like you to rescue me. Waiting for so many long, long nights."

His voice was filled with a sadness that struck her to the center of her soul. Never before had she ever heard such a lonely and desperate plea. Somehow she managed to calm herself enough to think. Although still breathing heavily, she decided to take advantage of his willingness to speak. She thought to use the time to gain her breath back in case she needed to run, before Tom had to come to her rescue. She kept a table between them, and constantly eyed back and forth between the headless man and the doorway out of the parlor. She was ready to bolt, inching her way toward freedom.

"One night, just one night a year I have hope," he began, his words dripping with sorrow and desperation. "My house becomes beautiful again. Everything is restored. Then, I wait in vain for someone kind enough to help me. Just one night... Please help me. My soul is unable to rest in peace until such a time that my head is returned to my shoulders."

Illustration by T. Glenn Bane.

Addie Mae listened as he spoke, her breathing relaxing, and her body becoming more at ease, as if the very sound of his voice were casting her into a trance. He told her of how, one fateful night long, long ago, he opened his house in hospitality to strangers, but in truth, they had tricked him and had planned all along to rob him of his hidden gold. Many times, in the days before the Revolutionary War, it was not wholly uncommon for a man to hide his wealth under a stone on his property, like under some steps or a hearthstone. He was fully prepared to just give them gold so they would leave and not harm his family or staff, but the situation quickly began to worsen and a fight broke out between the robbers and some of his servants. In the skirmish, one of the evil men pulled a sword off the wall. As the master of the house, he stepped in to protect his people, but an instant later his head was neatly sliced off. Sadly, his family was forced to bury him without his head, as they could not find where it had rolled. They left that same tragic night, never to return. The house sat empty and haunted. No one was able to live there while the wandering headless spirit sought its head.

Addie Mae was much calmer by the time the body had finished telling its horrific and sad tale. "Well, I would just love to help you, but I gotta get going," she said, as the headless body just stood there before her. "Remember, I told you, my husband is outside and he is very tall and very mean. I think I just…better…go."

But she couldn't. She could not find it in her to leave. The poor headless body of a man murdered stood before her, his hand outstretched still, imploring silently for her help. Maybe it was an odd compulsion, but she felt duty-bound to help him, as if some sort of magical force were being used against her. Addie Mae began to rationalize to herself that Tom would be along at any moment and whatever it was that the headless man would want her to do could not take so very long.

The headless gentleman, sensing that she was bending to his will, took a step closer to her. "Down the hall, under the winding staircase, is a small door that leads to the basement. I believe that is where my head is. You must help me get it back. Please, please, help me!"

Addie Mae looked down the long empty hallway, and yes, she did indeed see the small door that the headless man spoke of. She followed the ghost and together they left the room to calmly and quietly walk down the hall to the little door. As they neared it, as if by magic, its handle turned and the door swung open for them. With only a little hesitation, Addie Mae followed him down the steps. This was the only place in the whole house with no light, not even so much as a single candle. The stairwell was so dark, so eerie, and so terrifying. She almost lost her courage, but was too afraid to go back. She had to be careful as she descended the old, worn steps.

The creaky stairs led down into a dark, dank, musty-smelling blackness. The walls were lined with field stones and covered with slick moss. Spider webs hung thickly, brushing her face and hair... Addie Mae tried hard not to think about what sort of critter was making that scampering sound down near her feet.

The Gentleman Ghost was already at the bottom of the steps by the time she inched her way there. She could hardly see him; the only light down here was what had managed to trickle in from the brightly lit hall above. The cold and doom seemed about to swallow her, but luckily the Gentleman was hidden in the shadows. Addie Mae was able to pretend that it was darkness that hid his head from view.

She looked at him, where his eyes should have been, for some guidance as to what to do next. He did not speak, but rather pointed with a long, thin finger at a small shovel and then at the dirt floor.

Addie Mae did not need to speak. She inched her way over to the shovel and took it by the handle. The tool was icy cold to the touch and she almost dropped it in her surprise. She managed to hold on and with its tip broke into the hardened, old, compacted earth.

The room seemed to be getting colder and colder, and the shovel, which was already cold, added to the glacial chill that ran down her spine. Addie Mae was shaking so hard her teeth rattled. Digging at that hole was hard work made harder by the elements. Suddenly, she was not so confident she would be able to do this.

"Oh, maybe this won't take too much longer. My very soul is beginning to freeze," Addie Mae thought to herself. She dug and dug, just a little bit of dirt with each shovelful. The headless Gentleman stood motionless and watched her toil in the cold. With each shovelful the hole she dug grew deeper and wider.

Then, with the notable sound of metal hitting rock, a TWANG rang out in the dark and cold room. The Gentleman Ghost moved with such suddenness that it startled Addie Mae and she let a little shriek escape from her lips. She dropped the shovel and took several steps back, her hands groping in the dark behind her, feeling for the stairs.

Tom was still out walking the grounds looking for somebody. His concern about the unnaturally empty house was truly worrying him. Even the barn, the gatehouse — everywhere he looked was empty. Finally he saw a light, the dim glow of a lantern, and it was heading his way. Tom began walking, to meet it halfway. Desperate, scared, and cold, he hoped it was help.

There, in the meadow, was a farmer in his work clothes. "Howdy, stranger." He was kind looking and smiled when he spoke. "I reckon you'll be needing a place to stay with your wagon and all." He motioned with his lantern over toward Tom's team of horses. The friendly farmer nodded and with a knowing tone added, "You're best to be gone from here anyway. Come on over to my house. That place over there is not safe. This is the night of the haunting."

Tom's blood froze and he could only stare at the man. "I don't understand what you mean, 'the haunting?'"

The smile left the farmer's face but for a moment and he came closer to Tom, bathing him in more of the lantern's light. "You must not be from here. That house only appears one night a year. There are so many tales told about it. No one has been able to live there for years and years. The ghost that haunts it has no head. The stories 'bout it are awful. Who knows what terrible things happen to anyone who goes inside." Not wanting to frighten the young man any further, the farmer changed the subject. "Come on, you'll come to my house. My wife and I have an extra room. You can rest up and then we can even feed ya in the morning."

Eyes wide and slack jawed, Tom staggered back in shock. He was about to exclaim his disbelief in the whole matter when a banshee howl cut through the night like a knife. "Addie Mae!" Tom's voice was filled with dread. "That's my bride, she's in the house! Oh no! She fell asleep in there! We've got to help her."

The farmer and Tom took off like a pair of shots across the meadow, each hoping it was not too late to save the poor unfortunate girl.

The Gentleman Ghost fell to his knees and mantled over the hole. He stabbed his hands downward and as he drew them out, he rose to his feet, holding something. Addie Mae stared into the darkness, trying to tell what it was. Then, to her horror, she realized…it was a human skull.

Addie Mae could feel her body begin to swoon, and she did not want to faint, but there was a very real chance she was not going to have the option not too. Her senses reeling, the Gentleman Ghost turned and looked at her, and before her ever widening eyes, the skull began to restore itself into the visage that she had only imagined earlier. He stood before her headless no longer, but rather with chiseled good looked and was classically handsome.

"Thank you. Thank you so much." His voice was filled with so much joy and elation; it was the only thing that was keeping her conscious at this time. "Please, be the one to have my gold. It is under the step, the hearth step." With that final word, poor Addie Mae could stand it no longer. She wailed like a banshee and fainted dead away, hitting the floor in a heap.

The front door was as Tom had left it, wide open. He leaped over the threshold and raced into the parlor only to see it empty. He dashed out, back into the hall, and with his senses on a heightened alert, saw the small door he had missed before, still standing open.

He and the farmer ran down the hall, Tom charging down the steps and stopping only when he saw his poor little bride sprawled out on the floor. He called to her and not able to wait for a response, swooped down upon her, scooping her up in his arms. He was terrified that she was dead, and, calling her name repeatedly, he held and tried to rouse her.

The farmer caught up to him and bathed her face in the light of the lantern just in time for Tom to see her long, beautiful, black eyelashes flutter and open, revealing her eyes.

"Tom," she whispered, "Tom, it was so frightening and so awful." She had to pause as her husband tried to keep her from speaking, but she pressed on. "But I had to help the Gentleman, the man who owned this house all those years ago. No one would ever help him, but I did, and he gave me his gold."

Tom knew better than to try to keep his little Addie Mae from speaking so he just let her prattle right along as he continued to carry her. She told them both the tale of what happened as they left the house. They rushed out of there quickly and climbed in the wagon to get away. Tom followed the farmer to his house. With a glance back over his shoulder, Tom saw the lights in the mansion windows blinking out, one by one.

Once at the homestead, the farmer and his wife put them up in a cozy room. They were all so exhausted and no one tried to think too much about the wild and fanciful tale Addie Mae had spun. She slept fitfully, talking about it in her sleep, in her nightmares, between the screams.

The next morning, Addie Mae awoke appearing to be refreshed and restored to her usual self, although she did not speak of the events of last night. Tom figured that was for the best and planned that they would be leaving as early as possible after eating breakfast. He just looked up from his meal to ask for another cup of tea when he noticed that his wife was no longer at the table with them.

Tom ran to the window and saw his wife walking across the meadow, back toward that terrible house.

Hollering for the farmer, Tom rushed out of the house. The two of them raced across the meadow following the trail of trampled grass that Addie Mae had left in her wake.

When they came upon her, she had just reached what should have been the bottom of the marble steps they stood upon last night. Today, however, they were a pile of rubble. In fact, the entire house looked as if it had collapsed and folded in upon itself. There was nothing left of the opulent home; now it was all broken timbers, splintered remains of furniture, molded carpet remnants, and useless bits of glass or trinkets. The only bits of the memory of the house that still stood together were the many chimneys of the home's numerous fireplaces.

Tom reached out and grabbed Addie Mae, trying to stop her from going into the dangerous ruins, but she snapped her arm away. "Tom, he gave me the gold and I aim to retrieve it." Tom tried to stop her a second time, but she would not have it. She reached down and picked up a fire poker from the ground and ran to the hearthstone step with it.

Tom and the farmer went after her, but she was small and she made her way through the maze of debris fast. She worked as quickly as she could, knowing that at any second her husband and the kindly farmer might try to stop her, but Tom saw the fixed determination of his wife and decided to let her finish what she had started. Besides, after everything that had happened last night, he was curious now too. Lending a hand when she could do no more on her own, Tom and the farmer pried up the hearthstone step just enough for Addie Mae to take a peek at what was under it.

She made a happy sound and quick as a snake shot her hand under the stone and came back holding an old leather satchel. The men let the stone go, and when Addie Mae opened the flap, the aged leather fell apart, revealing numerous pieces of gold and releasing a shower of falling gold dust upon the hearthstone step.

Addie Mae was a good woman; she gave much of the gold to the Gentleman's surviving family and used the rest to give her and her husband a good start at life. In fact, they purchased the land that was near the friendly farmer and the Gentleman's old mansion home, but maybe the nicest thing they ever did with the gold was to buy and place a headstone befitting and worthy for the Gentleman Ghost and had it placed in the field out behind his old home.

Addie Mae's tale of what happened spread across the Uwharrie Mountains and soon folks from all over came to their home to see the old house and hear the story from Addie Mae for themselves. Folks even came from as far away as Greensboro.

As the years passed, Addie Mae never again heard or saw her generous Gentleman Ghost. However, there was this one time when she felt like she needed to be alone for a little while that she rode her own horse over to the old ruined home and walked in the field out back. It could have been the wind playing tricks on her, but even when she was a great-great-grandmother and lying on her deathbed surrounded by all her family and friends, she told the tale again and said that she heard on that day in the field someone whisper in her ear, "Thank you so much for helping me. I am now resting in peace."

Chapter Two:

Graveyards

Boneyard, burial ground, cemetery, graveyard, memorial park, necropolis — no matter what word you like to use, these places where we lay our dead to rest were perhaps early man's first permanent settlements. Oftentimes homes were constructed only to last a season, as ancient humans had to follow the herds and their migratory paths or move their houses each year because the rivers they lived along would rise and flood. Homes came and went, but the graves of those who died — their resting place — was as fixed and permanent as death itself.

Much of what we know about the past today is information that was collected and logically deduced from funerary artifacts, the items that we buried along with our dearly departed. Even in our modern times, it makes a kind of sense that if our beloved deceased are buried in their Sunday best with some of their personal belongings their spirits may linger about their eternal resting place. If there is any truth to this idea at all, that may explain why ghosts are said to be seen and experienced in graveyards across the country and why most graveyards have some sort of fence around them — not to keep folks out, but rather to keep the ghosts in.

Don't Leave Open the Graveyard Gate

"Don't leave open the graveyard gates"
"Don't leave open the graveyard gates"
"Don't leave open the graveyard gates"

Old graveyards on a nice sunny day can be peaceful places to spend an afternoon resting and exploring. They are really rich with history, stone art, statues, and gardens, but, in the dark of night, they're another story.

Now Jennie Sue and her mama lived in a pretty little cottage on a lane near the church and its graveyard. It was a very old place, that church and graveyard. It had a black iron fence all around, as was the custom back then.

Jennie's mama, she was a sweet lady, but she was ailing a little bit. She said, "Now, Jennie honey, you go on down the lane, and go see Granny Smith. She'll fix me up some of her healing herb tea or something soothing to make me feel better."

Jennie got on her cloak and hurried out the door. The darkness was falling and she wanted to make sure she was home before the dark came. She'd heard tales about that graveyard. Oh, she loved it during the day, but those big iron gates, they stayed closed at night. It was said that if the graveyard gates were left open at night, who knew what terrible things might come out of that graveyard. So Jennie checked them as she went by and noticed that yes, the gates were closed tight, but as she was walking, the rain started pouring down, the wind was blowing, and she was about to blow off the road. She hurried on up 'cause she hated storms and she sure didn't want to be out in this one by herself. She could hear the

Graveyard gates, like this one at Greensboro Historical Museum in Greensboro, are kept secure to keep wandering spirits in. *Photo by Cynthia.*

banging of thunder and the flash of lightning, and she shivered again inside her cloak.

When she got to Granny Smith's house, Jennie knocked on the door. Knock, knock, knock... The door opened — CREEAAK — and there was that sweet lady standing in the lamplight. "Come on in, precious. I got just what your mama needs. She needs some of my sweet herb tea. I'll fix her up just right. You need to hurry on down, Jennie Sue. That storm is getting worse. Why, they say it's hard to tell what will happen tonight."

So, after a quick drink and snack, Jennie Sue gathered up all the medicines from Granny Smith. She bid her good-bye and thanked her as she went on out the door.

By now, the lane was pitch-black dark. The only light you could see was the flash of the lightning. Jennie Sue was getting more and more frightened. As she got close to the graveyard, she hurried faster. The shadows were even deeper and darker and the trees' branches were stretched like wild, crazy arms ready to reach out and grab her. Jennie began to run faster.

She was almost to home when out of the sky there came a loud crash. The lightning hit a tree, one of those massive trees at the edge of the graveyard, and the tree fell with a loud crash across the fence, across the gate, and there right before her eyes she saw the gate open.

"Oh no," she thought, "I've got to do something. We can't leave that gate open all night. Even if there is a storm, I have to do something."

She put everything down and started pulling and pushing on that tree, trying to push it off the gate, but everything she tried was not enough. It was a big old tree and way too heavy for her to pick up.

Then she thought well, maybe, just maybe she could push the gate — and that's just what she did. She pushed it from the underneath side as hard as she could and, with a great big shove, she managed to click it right into place. Even though it was crooked, she knew that the graveyard gate was closed.

She gave a sigh of relief and went on home to her warm cozy house with her sweet, sweet mama waiting at the door. Mama gathered her up into a big hug and sat her by the fire for some warm cocoa while Jennie told her the whole frightening story.

Mama said, "Jennie Sue, I am very proud of you. You were a brave girl to do that, and now we know that everything is gonna be all right. I'm feeling better already...and we know that the graveyard gates are shut tight."

So, whatever you do...

"Don't leave open the graveyard gates"
"Don't leave open the graveyard gates"
"Don't leave open the graveyard gates"

Author's Note: Here's a favorite recipe of mine. It's called "Sweet Healin' Herb Tea."

- 2 tablespoons of chamomile leaves
- 2 tablespoons of fresh mint leaves
- 1 to 2 teaspoons of honey

Pour 1 cup boiling water over all this and steep for 6 minutes. If you're old enough and you like, you may add just a dash of good whiskey (for medicinal purposes only!).

Whistling in the Graveyard

Nellie walked home through the nice sunny graveyard on her way home from her best friend's house several times a week. It was a shortcut and she liked the marble stones and the statues and the pretty flowers. She'd heard that if you whistled when you walked through a graveyard that nothing strange could follow you home.

First Presbyterian Church's graveyard at the Greensboro Historic Museum.
Photo by Cynthia.

One day she was busy thinking about her boyfriend and all kinds of other things and, as she was walking, she forgot to whistle. Near the big old iron gates she got a funny feeling that somebody was following her...that somebody was there. When she whirled around, the path was deserted, but still she had a creepy feeling.

She ran as fast as she could through the gates and then on home. Breathlessly, she told her mama what had happened, and you know how mamas are, so strong and comforting. "Now Nellie, you know there is no such thing, darling. You get your homework finished and set the table for supper and just quit all that nonsense."

Unfortunately, just about that time her brother walked by and he started chanting, "Na na na na na, Nellie is a baby!" Oh, he made her mad. You know how brothers can be. So she forgot all about it — and him too hopefully.

After supper and some family storytelling, it was time for bed. Nellie started worrying and thinking. She finally said, "Mama, you think maybe I could leave the hall light on, you know, just for tonight?"

Her mama smiled and said, "Sure you can." They went on upstairs and she got ready for bed. Her mama smoothed that homemade quilt right over Nellie and her doll, but about that time, there he came again, her brother, running down the hall singing, "Na na na na na, Nellie is a baby!"

Mama told him to hush. Soon Nellie started thinking, and she finally said, "OK, Mama, go ahead and turn off the light."

The night was quiet as Nellie fell fast asleep, holding her teddy bear, all snuggled down in that nice soft quilt. The house got real quiet, and sometime around midnight, she woke up, and she sat up, and she listened. She'd heard a bang downstairs. Then, somebody was softly calling her name. "Nellie, oh Nellie."

She was so scared she could barely breathe. Then, she heard it again, a little bit closer this time. "Nellie, oh Nellie. I'm coming to get you, Nellie."

By now, Nellie was terrified. Something had followed her home from the graveyard. Something was coming to get her, here, right in her house. She wanted to scream, but she was too frozen with fear. She threw the covers over her and her doll and just lay there shaking, but still the terrifying voice came closer. "Nellie, I'm coming to get you, Nellie. I'm on the first step. I'm on the second step. I'm on the third step. I'm on the fourth step. I'm on the fifth step. I'm coming to get you. I'm on the sixth step. I'm on the seventh and eighth step. I'm coming in your door."

The door creaked open.

Nellie was holding her breath and shaking even harder when that door creaked open. Then, she heard the footsteps coming toward the bed. They were coming closer and closer and closer. And then, out of the darkness, "Gotcha!"

When she opened her eyes and screamed, there stood her awful brother laughing.

Mama, Daddy, and the dog all came a-running. Everybody was talking at once. Mama was fussing and Daddy was blowing steam. It took a while for everything to get calmed down so everybody could go back to sleep, but of course, with the lights on. Boy, did that ornery brother get in trouble. He had to do double chores for a week, could not seeing his friends, and he even had to tell Nellie that he was sorry about five times.

"Ha ha ha ha ha, ha ha, nanny nanny boomer."

Nellie still took the shortcut most days, but she always remembered to whistle and so should you!

Priscilla and the Colonel

The plantation was large and graceful with big regal white columns, a wide front porch, and elegant gardens. The Stevens lived there, and

What ghostly spirits does this cemetery hold? *Photo by Cynthia.*

Priscilla was their only child.

That Priscilla! She was well-known around there because she was spoiled rotten. Even as a child and then on into young adulthood, Priscilla wanted everything her way and got it! I mean everything.

Now the plantation was well-known for its beauty, and at the edge of the plantation, as was the custom, was an old burying ground. It was for the families thereabouts, and it was nice and neat with pretty flowers and a wrought iron fence all around. This graveyard, though, was particularly interesting — and everybody liked to come and wander through it because of all the old stories and graves.

One grave was extra odd and strange. Everyone knew the story: it was said that a Colonel from the Revolutionary War was buried in that old burying ground. Strangely enough, he had been buried, at his special request, standing straight up in his dress uniform. The legend surrounding him was that no one could possibly stand on the Colonel's grave, especially after night. For if you stood on his grave, it was said that he would reach on up and grab you and bring you on down — and nobody wanted for that to happen.

Well, it was a favorite spot for everyone to go, and at the plantation parties, why, the Stevens had grand parties. Everybody wanted to be invited to their parties. You could hear the music coming out across the lawn; you could see the graceful dances and the dresses swaying. The uniformed servants had delectable foods they were laying out, and the flowers were so gorgeous.

On the patio one evening, Priscilla was holding court, as she loved doing at one of these grand events. Oh, she was very beautiful, and of course her mama always got her the best clothes, the best dresses, with designs and materials right from Paris, France, and her shoes were handmade. You could tell with one look at her that Priscilla knew it — she thought that she was the best at everything. She thought that she was the prettiest and the smartest, and why, she even claimed to be the bravest, if you can believe that.

Priscilla, as usual, was showing off at the party. She was telling everybody some tale about how she had single-handedly saved her dear, sweet grandma from drowning in the sound. Nobody believed it; after all, everybody knows that Grannies don't go swimming in the sound.

As was the custom, though, everybody kinda put up with Priscilla, but on this night, they were tired of it. In fact, one of the young men was so tired of it he came up with an idea.

He said, "Priscilla, ya know, I am really, really not believing that story. And I am tired of hearing about all of this bravery you supposedly have. Why, I bet that you couldn't even bring yourself to go to the graveyard and stand on the Colonel's grave. I just think you're all talk. I don't think you're brave at all. Why, everybody knows about the

Colonel. That would be the perfect test for you, Priscilla. You could really show us then how brave you are."

There was a quietness in the group. You could hear the sweet and lovely music coming out from the ballroom. You could hear the clinking of glasses and see the firelight dancing, the lanterns and candles that cast a soft glow — and they showed Priscilla's face. She was dead quiet.

What was she gonna do? She had boasted and bragged until now she was going to have to do something to prove it. She started in with, "Well, my daddy doesn't allow me to go to the burial ground this time of night, you ought to know that."

Everybody just looked at her. So the young man said again, "Well, are you going to go or not? Because if you don't go, we're not going to believe any more of these stories you keep telling us about being so brave and all."

Priscilla's perfect curls trembled, and I must say, a little bit so did she. The ball gown with its big ruffled skirt was not the kind of thing you'd be wanting to wear walking across that damp and dewy green lawn toward the burying ground, but that's just what she had to do.

She gulped and took a deep breath and then said, "All right. Ahem, I reckon I could go just for, you know, a little while. My papa wouldn't have to know. And then I could come right back. Why, I bet you a five-dollar gold piece that I can go and spin on that old Colonel's grave."

Everybody laughed a little bit, knowing a five-dollar gold piece was nothing to her, but the boys — those young men were smart. One of them said, "All right, Priscilla, it's a bet. But, you have to take your daddy's sword. You know the one, from the war, and stick it right in the ground. Otherwise how are we gonna know that you actually stood on the Colonel's grave? Cause you're going alone."

Alone? Alone! She hadn't thought she was gonna have to go alone, but, she was on the spot and she had to do it. So one of the young men went in the house. He got the sword that was her father's ceremonial sword from the war and brought it and a lantern out and gave them to Priscilla.

The whole group watched in silence as she slowly walked across that dewy wet grass. You could see the lantern swinging back and forth as she walked, trembling a little bit, she claimed from the cold, but they knew otherwise.

She finally walked that long, long distance. They were still there on the patio, watching and waiting.

Watching and waiting.

They heard it through the night, above the music, the creaking of that gate as she opened it wide. Then they saw the lantern again going into the darkness. It was waving back and forth, back and forth just a little bit by now. They could picture her walking in between all those graves, the ones from fifty years ago, the old, old graves, some of them a little bit newer, and then, toward the back of the graveyard — that's when they saw the lantern stop. They knew by now she was near that tall, marble, arched tombstone of the Colonel. A big memorial had been placed there by some of his relatives and friends, and it was quite grand. They could picture her standing there, getting ready to step on the grave.

There was a hushed silence. Luckily none of the adults had come out to the patio. The small group stood, just watching and waiting, waiting on the lantern to begin its journey coming back to the patio. That's when it happened. Soundlessly, the lantern went out — and the graveyard was touched in total darkness.

Then they heard it... They heard a horrible, terrifying scream. They knew... They knew it was Priscilla.

As fast as they could, they ran across that grass. Some of the boys were faster, of course, and by now the parents had heard too and were coming out onto the porch and wanting an explanation of what was happening, but the young people were already almost to the graveyard. They threw open the other gate, they went there through the graveyard with all of their lanterns waving back and forth faster, and then there they stopped.

The shiny marble of the Colonel's grave was glistening in the darkness. They looked down, not knowing what they'd find — and indeed, it was the worst. Because there, lying on the ground — the *cold, cold* ground — was Priscilla. Her dress all spread out with some of the petticoats torn and tattered, she looked white as a sheet. They thought she was dead.

Quickly, someone came and lifted her up to see if she was indeed dead, but she wasn't. She was still breathing. Ah, there was a sigh of relief from all. At about that time the adults had gotten to the gate of the graveyard — and they figured out immediately what was going on.

Her papa raised her up and said, "Speak to me, my darling. Are you OK, my precious Priscilla?"

They had to get Priscilla out of the graveyard. As they were pulling her up and lifting up her skirts, her daddy was getting ready to carry her, but he couldn't get her up in his arms. Something, something was holding her skirt to the ground.

Everyone stopped and froze. One woman screamed and fainted because they were sure that the legend was true: the Colonel had reached up and grabbed hold of Priscilla and was now at this instant holding her tight.

Her papa almost dropped her. Some of the men held up the lantern so that they could see the skirt and sword shining in the light. It was then that they discovered that Priscilla had taken the sword and stomped it into the ground, but when she did she put it right through her French dress and her petticoats and everything. So it wasn't the Colonel's long, skeletal fingers holding her to the ground. Instead, it was because she put that sword right through her own dress.

Well... when everybody realized what had happened, why, they started laughing and having a good joke. Papa picked her up and took her right on back up to the house and of course a big fuss was made about her.

After some rest and pampering, Priscilla was all right. In fact, everyone all along the whole coastal village was talking about it. She kinda liked being so important, but she wasn't very happy about being laughed at.

Ya know, from that day on, Priscilla stopped bragging. She stopped being so spoiled. It was as if the Colonel, even though he hadn't snatched her, had helped her grow up.

✝✝✝✝✝

Now you too might like to go explore some of these graveyards. There are many up and down the coasts of North and South Carolina that are very old, interesting, and have many legends about strange buryings, as they say. Whatever you do, though, be sure that you don't leave open the graveyard gates!

Taken in Summerfield, North Carolina on Pleasant Ridge Road. *Photo by Cynthia.*

Chapter Three:

Greensboro

The "Gate City"

Settlers first began trickling into the area during the 1740s to lay claim to their stakes and tend to farms, and in 1771 Guilford County was officially established. Greensborough was planned to be the county seat, as it was geographically centralized and easy to reach from any part of the county. The courthouse and town square were established in 1808, and everything else grew up around it. The town was named to honor the American Revolution War hero, Major General Nathanael Greene, who commanded the American Continental troops at the Battle of Guilford County Courthouse. The town developed at a slow and steady pace until Governor Morehead was able to win a railroad grant in the 1840s. Soon Greensborough became the transportation hub for the state, thereby earning itself the nickname "The Gate City."

After the Civil War, brothers Caesar and Moses Cone developed their large-scale textile mills in Greensborough — it was their industry that turned this slow-growing, sleepy village into a growing city in just under ten years. In 1895, the city changed its name to "Greensboro" and was considered to be the center of the southern textile industry. During the 1920s real estate boom, Greensboro was called "the wonder of the state." Even during the Depression era, the city hardly seemed to notice. Starting in 1940 and lasting well into the 1960s, the city continued to prosper — it was the world's largest supplier of denim and many companies had built their corporate offices here.

Today, all 109 square miles of Greensboro is home to some 240,000 hard-working folks, making it the largest city in the county, the county seat, and the third largest in the state. It's located between Interstates 40, 71, and 85, making it easy to get to no matter where you may be coming from...just like its founders would have wanted.

Blandwood Manor

Many years ago, back when I was a librarian, I worked in the downtown Greensboro branch. On my lunch break, one place I liked to visit was the charming, historic graveyard of the Greensboro Historic Museum. In fact they held the first of the thirty years of "Ghost Stories in the Grave Yard" with me there around then.

Another intriguing place downtown to visit was Governor John Motley Morehead's mansion, Blandwood. (Morehead was in office 1841-1845.) Back then, like now, it sat atop a lush green hill like a beautiful yellow gem aglow in the sun.

Before my lunchtime visits to the restored mansion I never knew its history. I learned about it through the tours we went on and candlelight Christmas events that I attended there. The more I learned about the mansion, the more fascinating it became. For instance, a part of Blandwood is the oldest house in Greensboro that is still using its original foundation. I learned that before it was restored in recent years; it had sat for a long time, deteriorating into a rundown looking place. They say it looked more like a haunted house than the stately manor it is now.

The grounds and gardens have been restored to loveliness again. There are several old trees said to be at least 175 years old. A large, graceful Willow Oak is 200 or more years old. It is a peaceful quiet retreat. Sitting in the garden you almost feel transported back in time.

Blandwood Manor. *Photo by Theresa Bane.*

Governor Moorehead's memorial, located in the First Presbyterian Church's graveyard at the Greensboro Historical Museum. *Photo by Cynthia*.

When we got married in 1980, Fred and I decided that we wanted to have a fun wedding dance and party at the Blandwood Carriage House. I was still working downtown. Growing to love the Manor, I felt a connection to it, so we enjoyed an evening candlelight gala with music, dancing, and good food with friends and family. It was a magical evening to remember.

Letita

Through the decades Fred and I have continued to visit Blandwood Manor. Recently, Ashley Poteat, its executive director, had an inspired idea: an October storytelling in the parlor of Blandwood. Our first event was such a success I have told friendly ghostly tales there for several years since. There are of course many tales told about strange happenings in the house. I decided to include here some of my fictional stories. One of the ones I created features my favorite lady of the house: Letitia, Governor Morehead's daughter.

Governor Morehead's daughter, Letitia, had come back home to Blandwood with her children. A lovely, refined lady she was quite the hostess for the many gathers at the manor. When she had a chance, it was said that she like to go up in the impressive tower that's located in the front of the home to spend time there. The view was beautiful making it a tranquil place for reading or reflection. Back then, Blandwood was not in the busy center of downtown Greensboro with its tall buildings and crowds of people. Since those days, the town has grown up all around it. Perhaps on some evenings, Letitia would go to the tower with a lighted candle leading the way. It was said that a candle could be seen for miles, a strange, eerie light.

Letitia loved Blandwoood so much that she is said to haunt the tower even now. She later moved away and lived happily ever after. BUT! Her spirit continues to linger at the mansion. There are nights where folks say that you can see the light of a flickering candle in the highest window of the tower. Some say there's even a shadow of a lady!

Letitia's children were by all accounts very happy there during their time at the manor. It's said that sometimes, if you are downstairs in the parlor, you can hear the sound of little footsteps running above you. Her children had their own playroom in the manor and spent many a joyful afternoon there. One afternoon more recently, a visitor was touring the lovely home with two friends. They paused a moment in the sunlight-filled parlor to admire the chandelier and antiques. Suddenly they were startled to hear children laughing, the sounds over head of a ball bouncing, and then the running of small feet. Startled, they heard giggling as well, just as if children were upstairs playing.

The ladies immediately called one of the docent tour guides. By the time she had gotten to the parlor, there was nothing but empty silence. The ladies insisted they be shown the overhead room immediate! After climbing the steps, the group found just another lovely restored room — no children and no games. Their guide was not surprised. She explained that others had experienced the same happenings. You see, that room had been a playroom for Letitia's family decades ago. During some of the Christmas tours, the director Ashley Poteat and her staff will tell you of the Victorian Christmas games those children loved in that same room.

Strange Occurrences

Another tale is about the antique clock that stands in the front hall of Blandwood. It has not worked in many years. Even though a few repairmen have attempted to fix it, the clock just simply will not keep time. The one thing it will do like clockwork, however, if you will pardon the pun, is keep its glass door open. Every time it is shut, as soon as you turn your back to it, the door will swing wide open. Folks who work there have tried to keep it closed in various ways, but nothing has worked. A group stood in the parlor one afternoon, listening to the tour guide's information. The guide was interrupted by the startled group gasping in surprise as the glass door of the clock swung open right before their very eyes! They were lucky enough to have quite an extra exciting tour.

These are not the only stories of ghosts in Blandwood Manor. You'll hear many other stories. One of them is about a spirit that everyone supposes is a gentleman. No one knows who he was or why he haunts the home, but he has shown a definite preference for the ladies. Usually only they can hear him creaking his way up the steps that lead to the offices. They can hear him banging his way down the hall, stomping as he goes. Then he begins to pace back and forth, back and forth. When they open the door, there is no one there! The hallway is empty! Sure enough, though, sooner or later they'll hear him coming up those steps again and making his way down the hall — and every time they get up to look to see who it is there is never anyone there. The Gentleman of Blandwood gets his attention anyway he can.

†††††

Though these accounts have not been proven to be fact, Blandwood Manor is open for tours if you want to experience it for yourself. Tour the house and gardens. Look in the shadows as well as the dark corners. Maybe you will encounter a spirit of your own. Better still, you can have your own party in the carriage house and experience the beauty of Blandwood. Remember to look back at the tower — maybe you too will see a flickering candle.

Jane Aycock

When I first came over from the coast to go to college at the University of North Carolina at Greensboro, the school was still predominantly a lady's school. My father had wanted me to attend a lady's school because his thinking was that I would get my teaching certificate sooner and without the distractions of "boyz" as he would say, and without all of the parties that he knew other universities had.

Well... at that time there was only about five or six hundred "boyz" from around Greensboro who attended the school. Now the university is a huge, sprawling, well-known, big old school. It has continued to grow and spread. Even the house that I had lived in at one point is now gone, replaced by a parking lot.

Photo by Theresa Bane.

You can still go to Yum-Yum Ice Cream and have lunch. It's a place that brings back a lot of memories for so many folks. They get a pretty big crowd there on a Saturday. Being there and thinking back, it's sometimes hard to believe the mysteries that happened there at the university.

North Spencer Dormitory was one of the very first built for the school. It's two stories, and has what looks like a bell tower on it. Yes, the building is still there; you can drive by the school and see it for yourself. You can even stop and go look at it, but those who have lived in North Spencer know the truth about it. For you see, North Spencer is haunted.

When I lived in North Spencer, that was one of the first things I heard in the dorm. There were lots of stories about it. We would go and look every night for the ghost; we'd walk outside and look up at the tower, as that was where you were supposed to be able to see the ghost — a poor, sad girl.

You see, one of the early lady students at the Women's College, that's what UNCG was known as back then, had been disappointed in love and because of it, they say, she took her own life up there in the tower. Now, they say, her spirit haunts the tower.

Us girls, we'd watch and wait and try to see if we could see anything — a movement, a shadow, even a light. Maybe there were too many of us girls there at one time and too much giggling happening, but I never did see anything. I have always felt that had I been able to climb up those stairs, as they were closed back then and still are now I'm sure, that I could have gone up there and may have been able to feel her presence. Or see her shadow or her light. Unfortunately, I never did get to do so.

Recently, however, I've talked to some students. The dorm is still a popular place to live because it's older and mysterious and historic. The stories are still told about the spirit that haunts old North Spencer Dorm. So if you drive by on a night very slowly, on a night when there are not so many people out and about, look up at the tower and see if you can't see the spirit of the poor, sweet college girl that is still up there, trying to find her love.

Aycock Auditorium

Around the corner from North Spencer Dorm is where Ms. Jane Aycock's house used to be. The university bought it from her back then because they wanted to build a big, beautiful, fancy theater. Greensboro didn't have anything like that back then and so they decided to name it after her, calling it Aycock Auditorium.

Ms. Jane Aycock was said to have been a little bit strange and a little bit peculiar. She had apparently gotten very angry they had taken her house and she told everybody that it wasn't even her idea to sell the property. Nevertheless, the school built the theater and it was indeed big and beautiful. Oh, the plays and the music and the happiness that it brought to others. Some folks say that toward the end, Ms. Aycock changed her mind, softened up a little bit, and after attending a few productions there, decided that she liked it after all.

She may have liked it so much that some say she may never left. Oh, Aycock Auditorium is still there all these years later, but there are the whispered rumors that say the building is haunted. There have been many witnesses to these hauntings. Some just laugh it off while others refuse to come forward, but the music majors, the theater majors, and a whole variety of people have experienced the spirit of Ms. Jane.

One such man, a professor, had an experience there, and it's a fairly commonly told tale on the campus. He had been in Aycock Auditorium working late on a production. When he finally left, he realized that he had forgotten his briefcase and went back in to get it. When he was inside, he saw the lights of the stage, the footlights, snap on all by themselves. He rushed over to his briefcase, grabbed it, and as he left, turned to look over his shoulder back at the stage. It was there that he saw a shadow standing over toward the edge of the stage. He called out to it, but there was no answer. With that, he ran right out of the theater.

He's retired now and doesn't put on production plays any longer, but to this day, he is still not sure what happened or what he saw. Was it the spirit of Jane Aycock?

Other people have had similar experiences. It is said that if you are there in a totally lit-up theater after everyone else has left, the floodlights and the overhead chandelier suddenly snap off, plunging you into total

North Spencer Dormitory on the campus of University of North Carolina, Greensboro. *Photo by Theresa Bane.*

DARKNESS. With no logical explanation of what just happened or of how long the event will last, just as panic is about to set in, the lights suddenly come back on all by themselves.

Aycock Auditorium... Is it haunted? Well, you can hear doors CREAKING open and then shutting by themselves. The theater majors, actors, and actresses who work there can tell you that they experience a feeling like someone is combing their hair as they are putting on their costumes. When they whirl around, no one is in the room.

Is Jane Aycock still visiting her beloved theater? Who knows, but if you visit Aycock Auditorium and linger after everyone else has left, stay to see if you can meet the famous and lovely Jane Aycock yourself.

Chapter Four:

Jamestown

Founded in 1816 and named in honor of James Mendenhall, Jamestown is the earliest continuing settlement in the Piedmont. In fact, archeologists have evidence of human habitation dating back thousands of years. The Keyauwee Indians were living here in 1701, but they relocated south during the 1760s and were ultimately absorbed into the Catawba tribe.

Quakers from Pennsylvania came into the region looking for rich farmland and among those original settlers was James Mendenhall, who established his homestead in 1762. It was his son, George, who founded the village and named it in honor of his father. It was a bustling settlement with a Freemason's Lodge, an inn, and post office even before the gold was discovered. Jamestown was a "stop" along the Underground Railroad and during the Civil War its residents largely refused to fight for either side opposing the war and violence; instead, its residents made shoes and helped slaves escape to the North.

Jamestown incorporated in 1947 and began to develop a water and sewer system. T. C. Ragsdale, Sr., was the town's first mayor and as a testament to its stability of community its only had five other mayors since then.

Lydia

In the pines, in the pines
Where the sun never shines
Where the cold and the chilly wind blows

True love, true love don't 'cha lie to me
Tell me where you were last night???

In the pines, in the pines
Where the sun never shines
And the cold and the chilly wind blows

The falling sheets of rain made driving difficult for Jim as he drove home late one night. The road through Jamestown was narrow and dangerous even in the best of weather. There were no other cars on that lonely stretch of road near that railroad bridge. But just then, up ahead, right on the curve of the road, Jim thought he saw something. Yes, yes there was something. Rather *someone* is right there standing beside the road. Jim could hardly believe his eyes. Standing there in the rain and swirling fog was what appeared to be a, well, a lady, all alone. She stood there wearing nothing but a long, filmy dress. Her scarf and hair were blowing wildly in the cold wind.

"Lydia's Bridge"... After all these years a young accident victim is still trying to get home. *Photo by Theresa Bane.*

He quickly brought the car to a screeching stop. Jim jumped out into the rain and ran back to where he thought she stood. His greeting to her blew away in the stormy wind. Even in the darkness he could see that she was a beautiful young lady, but she was so pale though, so very pale. Her blond hair was wet and tangled in the wind. Her long gown looked like a party dress. However, it and the scarf she wore with it were tattered, dirty, and torn as they blew around in the cold wind, exposing her bare feet.

Wordlessly, she walked to his car. Jim rushed to open the back door. She glided past him to sit in the back seat. When she passed him, Jim felt a chill rush through his body, an eerie and strange feeling. He shook it off and reached in to get a blanket his grandmother had knitted to put over the lady, trying to warm her. Jim got in the car and started it back up. When he did, he turned around to face his new passenger and ask her where it was that he could take her. Still silent, she extended one pale thin arm and then pointed with one long bony finger toward a hill just up ahead, just past the curve in the road.

Jim drove slowly through the storm trying to see the road as the relentless rain made it difficult. He noticed that the temperature in his car was growing colder and colder. Even when he turned up his old heater, he found that he was still chilled to the bone. He drove on and, up ahead, he thought he saw a light. Yes, yes, there it was again, a light. There on the hill ahead was a quaint cottage barely visible in the fog and darkness, one that he had never seen before.

Slowly he drove the car up the drive to the little home and when he was close to the front door stopped the car. He got out and went around to open the door for his mysterious lady and when he did — AAHHH — the back seat was empty! Yes, empty! The cold fog swirled around him as he stared at the darkness that filled his back seat. She was gone! Where was she? He whirled around but saw only the foggy darkness.

"Well," Jim thought to himself, "perhaps she had gotten out and walked quickly into her house? Yes, that was it; she was already inside." Even as he said the words to himself, though, Jim couldn't stop this strange feeling he was having. He knew it could not be true, but yet he had to go up to that house, he had to make sure that the poor young lady had made it home.

He walked up the hill through the storm to the dimly lit old house. Once he was there on the porch, he could see through a window that there were some lights still turned on in the front room. He figured someone was still awake, so he knocked — KNOCK, KNOCK, KNOCK, KNOCK — and when he did, the knocking sound echoed out into the night as he waited for someone to answer.

Was She Just a Phantom?

After what felt like an endless period of time, the door slowly CREEAAKED open and there, in the shadows of the doorway, appeared a small and bent older lady. She looked at Jim, into him it seemed, and with a hollow greeting motioned for him to come inside her home. Jim explained to her he had picked up a young lady on the road who seemed to want to come to this house. Slowly, shaking her head, the elderly lady turned toward a lace-covered table. From it, she picked up a framed photograph and held it out for him to see. A quick glance showed Jim an image of a pretty young lady in a white ball gown.

"This," the old woman said in a small voice filled with pure sadness, "is my beautiful Lydia. She's been dead fifty years tonight. You see, I knew you'd come. For every year on this night, the anniversary of her death, and just this night alone, some nice young man such as yourself tries to bring my Lydia home. Again and again and again they try, each and every year. Thank you for trying too."

Jim stared at the old woman and shook his head slowly in disbelief. Then, with the sudden realization of what the old woman had just said, Jim cried out, "No! I saw her. I had her in my car. This isn't possible... Bring her out. What kind of cruel trick is this?"

At a loss for anything else he could say or do, Jim looked down at the picture he still held in his hands and really looked at it. When he did, he screamed — AAAHHH! — and instinctively let go of it, letting it fall to the floor. He could do nothing else because there in the photo was his very own mysterious passenger, the old woman's daughter, Lydia.

Photo by Cynthia.

Lydia's mother returned the photo to its place on the table and gathered a cloak around her frail old shoulders. She lit a lantern, gently took Jim by the hand, and led him out of the house. The pale and faint light of the lantern barely lit the way as they traveled outside into the darkness. Jim let the old woman lead him down a little path toward a small garden surrounded by a dark wrought iron fence. They came to the heavy gate doors which creaked when opened. Just past the gated fence Jim was able to see that he was not in a garden at all, but rather a small family graveyard. The fog here was thick and there were many shadows, but he was able to see what the old woman had led him to. Before him stood a small marble gravestone, carved with simple letters. It read "Lydia." Then, to his horror, Jim saw his blanket lying on the grave.

Some folks say that even to this day on a dark, foggy, rainy night, you too might see Lydia waiting, just waiting for someone to stop and give her a ride home — again.

††††††

Folks in Jamestown take their "Lydia" very seriously. She's a real local favorite. The railroad bridge and that section of road have been bypassed but they are frequently visited. Hopefully by the time you read this, you can visit the proposed little park and benches near the new highway marker sign that will show even to visiting strangers to Jamestown where the famous folktale events took place back in the 1930s.

The Woman With the Basket

Old Mendenhall Plantation in Jamestown, North Carolina, is haunted, or so they say. Like many of the old home places, the ghosts and spirits of the past are still there, some for happy reasons and some for not. When you visit the plantation house, don't forget to ask about the story of the lady with the basket. The story goes that you can see her just about dusk as she is heading off to the barn. They say that the woman with the basket at Mendenhall Plantation is a nice and harmless ghost, most likely the eldest of the Mendenhall daughters, Minerva, off to collect eggs. Still... if you should see her, do be careful because maybe, just maybe she'd like some company and help with her basket like the ghost in this story.

Tom and Jim were best friends ever since they were children. Now that they were older and had their own places, they still liked to visit each other whenever they could. They lived in a small village and would take turns going back and forth between each other's home. Even as adults

Mendenhall Plantation in Jamestown, North Carolina.
Photo by Theresa Bane.

they did everything together. They would spend their evenings sitting by the fire, telling stories, whittling wood, and chewing on their corncob pipes as they enjoyed one another's company.

As it happened Jim would usually lose track of time and stay later at Tom's house than he'd mean to. It was usually Tom who had to remind him when it was getting late, but on this one particular evening he didn't. They had been having an especially good time. It was nearly midnight before Tom noticed the time. Typically Jim just would have left, but it was cold and foggy out so Tom tried to get his friend to spend the night.

"It's too late to be out traveling, too cold too," he said to his friend. "Why don't you spend the night? My family and girlfriend are not coming till tomorrow so there's nothing going on; it won't matter to them. It's too late to go. Just stay over and leave first thing in the morning."

Jim just shook his head. "No, no, I want to get home. I miss my dog and I need to feed him something and let him out. It's just that I need to leave, not that I don't want to stay."

Tom bid his friend good night and Jim went out the house and through the creaking front gate with his bright lantern. Closing the gate securely behind him, he set off down the long, curvy, rambling mountain road toward home.

It was a cold night and there was just a hint of a moon visible up in the sky, making the night all that much darker. Even though a fog had settled, Jim could just make out that there was someone else walking on the road up ahead of him. He slowed his pace down and wondered who would be out at this late hour besides himself. Not wanting to make the long walk by himself and liking the idea of having a little company, he picked his pace back up and caught up to the stranger. As he began to draw nearer, the figure began to take on a clearer form until quite to his surprise he was able to see that it was an elderly lady. She wore an old-fashioned cloak around her shoulders, and as she walked she did so sort of bent over as if she were carrying something heavy.

As Jim got closer to her, he spoke out so that he would not frighten her. "Good evening, ma'am," he said as politely as he knew how. "Cold night. Mind if I carry your basket for you?"

The old woman was very quiet; in fact, she didn't even say a word in response to Jim. By now, the moon that was just a sliver to begin with was hidden behind some clouds, making the night even darker than it already was. The fog had all but hidden the road and, although he knew the road well that led to his home, Jim was beginning to get a strange feeling come over him.

The old woman continued walking down the dark and winding road, and Jim kept up with her. He chatted politely to her, even though she never did say a word back to him. He asked her a few times "Why are you out so late?" but she never would answer him. He supposed she had her reasons, but it did worry him that she — a small and bent old woman — was carrying such a heavy basket. He asked her again, "Ma'am, may I please carry your basket?"

The old woman stopped walking and without so much as looking at him, extended her arm and passed her basket over to him. Just as Jim was about to take it in his hands, the wind blew just a little and that little was just enough for it to move the cloth that was covering the top of it. When the cloth fanned back, Jim took a peek inside the basket and there he saw a head — AAAHHH!

Jim screamed, letting the basket drop to the ground. When it hit the road, the head that was carefully hidden within fell out, bounced on the ground, and began to roll. Still the woman said nothing, but Jim had already started running as fast as his legs could carry him. He lit off down the road, back the way he had come, toward his friend Tom's house. He ran fast and hard, recklessly looking over his shoulder every few steps to see if that old woman or the head was following him. He couldn't tell for certain; the fog was thick and closed in behind him as fast as he parted it. His eyes were peeled wide open, looking for any bit of movement. He could still see that head clearly in his mind.

When he finally reached Tom's house, he didn't bother trying to open that creaking old gate, but rather made a running jump right over it. He hardly touched the few stairs that led to the front door, but as soon as he reached it, he began pounding on it with both fists, hollering for his friend to open the door. The moment Tom did, Jim pushed past him and slammed the door tight, fixing the thick bolt lock into place himself.

Panting heavy and full of fear, he grabbed Tom by the shoulders and looking him in the eye said, "You are not going to believe what just happened to me, but it's true!" He took a quick look over his shoulder to make sure the door was firmly closed and locked in place before he continued. "There was an old woman and she had a basket with a severed head in it. Oh, gosh, I think she's still out there, I think she's out there right now. Look out the window and tell me what you see!"

Tom was thunderstruck for a moment, but then he just chuckled to himself. "Oh, Jim, I bet you just imagined the whole thing." He stepped around his lifelong friend and walked over to the window. He parted the curtain and still laughing a little, took a look outside. No sooner had he done so than he stopped laughing altogether. There, on the other side of his gate, stood a bent old woman holding tightly in her hands a heavy-looking basket.

So, if ever you should be walking alone one cold and foggy night on a curving mountain road and you should happen upon a stranger, take a moment to think before you stop. Especially before you offer to carry their basket.

The Gold in the Lake

Old Sam McCall was a very lazy man. In fact, he was probably the laziest man that anybody around knew. He was so lazy that his wife, Emmie Jo, could not even get him up off the couch for nothing. He'd just lie there all day long doing nothing, dozing off; there wasn't even TV to watch back then. Now back in those days folks had to work even harder than we do now, as nothing came prepackaged or ready-made. Everything was done by hand. Emmie Jo was always after her husband saying things like "You've got to get a job. If you don't get a job, we are not going to have anything in this here little house of ours."

Back in those days, the "olden times" as we like to call them, working for a living was hard work indeed, as it meant toiling all day with your hands and stressing your back. Knowing this all too well, Old Sam especially didn't want to get a job doing anything. He didn't want to work at all. So one day when his wife got after him for being lazy, he said, "Ya know, Emmie Jo, there's supposed to be some gold hidden down by the old mine, you know, down by the millpond. I think I'm gonna go down there and start looking for it. Nobody's searched lately and I bet that gold is just sitting there a' waiting for me to find it."

Emmie Jo let out a long, sad sigh and rolled her eyes at her husband. "Oh, you old fool," she said. "You know there is no such

The old Guilford Mill opened back in the 1700s and is still in operation to this day. If you visit the mill you can purchase flour that was processed right there. *Photo by Cynthia.*

thing as that lost gold down at the millpond." She didn't think it was a good idea for him to go waste his time with such foolishness. She wanted her husband to have a regular and honest job. "Besides," she continued, "haven't you heard that it's haunted? You're gonna go down there and get scared outta your boots."

"Oh, I ain't afraid," said Old Sam, dismissing his wife's words with a wave of his hand. "I'll be just fine, you watch'a. I'll bring you back a whole bunch o' gold."

So, Old Sam took up his bucket and got a hoe for raking out of his shed. He got into his hardly used bib overalls and work boots. And when he got everything on and ready, he went on out the front door and marched on down the long and raggedy gravel road toward the old millpond. Back in those days, roads weren't paved much, or well, and they didn't run all too straight either. It was going to be a long walk.

When Old Sam got down to the old pond, it was a nice day, cool and sunny, and, inspired, he started right in working. He started digging in the mud with the hoe. He started working hard. He started pushing that grown-up grass aside. He even started panning in the water a little bit. You know what that is, right, panning for gold? Oh yeah, they used to pan for gold all the time right here in North Carolina. Why, we were the country's first gold rush location…but back to Old Sam. He got himself a pan and was trying to sift it in the dirt and water and see if he got any gold out of the mud of the pond.

Well, he worked all day long. This was not what he liked doing, as it was not just work but hard work at that. "Aww," Old Sam thought to himself, "I just can't go home with nothing. I'm gonna have to try just one more time." So, Old Sam took only a short rest and ate a little snack and then went back at it. He was determined that he was going to find that gold and prove Emmie Jo wrong.

Back to work he went. He was so intent on his digging round about in the cattails and sea grass, and walking around in the water, that he didn't even notice that the old mill wheel was slowly going around and around. No one had worked in that mill for a long, long time, so no one was inside letting it spin. Old Sam was so focused on what he was doing that he almost didn't notice that darkness had started falling. Now he was not a man to be afraid of the night, but he didn't like being out there where it was so deserted all by himself.

So, almost begrudgingly, Old Sam packed up his hoe and pans and other stuff and much to his surprise saw that it was getting real dark real fast. It was one of those late fall days when the dark just seems to come out of nowhere and he thought to himself, "I got to be getting home to Emmie Jo."

As he was turning around to get the last of his stuff out of the water — that's when he saw it. Over there, a light, just like it was hanging from a tree. A lantern. It was swaying back and forth a little bit in the breeze. Old Sam blinked his eyes and, unsure of exactly what he was seeing, cried out, "What in tarnation is that! Hey, who's there? What are ya doing?"

There was no answer.

"Hello?"

There was still no answer. He knew just about everybody in these here parts and everybody knew him for the lazy thing he was, so the fact that nobody answered him when he called out got him even more worried. He hurried on up out of the water, his arms laden with his tools, and turned back around to take one last look as he was ready to hit the road. That's when he saw it — the lantern was close. It was, like, real close. And, and... why, it looked like it was coming toward him!

"AGGHH!" he screamed. Old Sam dropped his bucket and took off running fast and hard down that old raggedy road. He was running so fast that he ran right out of his boots. He ran and ran and ran... He even ran right out of his bib overalls. He ran like a deer all the way home. He ran right up to his own front door and immediately began beating on it, trying to get in.

"Let me in! Let me in, Emmie Jo! Hurry up! They're coming after me! Hurry up, if ya don't the ghosts are gonna get me! Open this door!"

When Emmie Jo did open the door, her husband fell right in the house — POW! — and landed flat on the floor. She just shook her head and looked down at him and started laughing. She said, "Sam, where are your boots? And what happened to your britches?"

Panting, Old Sam scrambled to his feet. He said, "You're not gonna believe it, Emmie Jo. You're just not gonna believe it, but they were out there! They had a ghost lantern and the ghosts were ready to grab me and pull me back and take me with them. You are just lucky, woman, that I am still among the living!" Panting hard and still excited he went on, "Quick, lock the door and look out the window. They're still out there... See for yourself. See if you don't see a ghost lantern!"

Emmie Jo looked out the front door. She didn't see anything unusual. She closed the door and locked it anyway, just like her panicked husband wanted. Then she went over to the window, pulled the curtain back, and looked outside, just like her husband said to. Again, she didn't see anything, but she did start laughing at him. "You have got to be the silliest and laziest man in this whole town. Why I ever married for love instead of money I'll never know. I guess I always knew that my mother was gonna be right." She sighed and put on her apron. "Well, Sam, come on in here and I'll fix ya some supper. And don't you ever go down by that lake again; you are just full of such foolishness."

And so it was... He listened to his wife finally. Old Sam never went back down to the old millpond and he had to get a regular old-time job. But, you need to beware, for in Guilford County, we have Castle McCulloch, an old abandoned gold mine — and we have several mills, including Guilford Mill, which still works to this day, grinding grains like it always has, by water. Could it be that that part of the story is true? Could it be that there are spirits there, waiting, waiting for darkness, waiting for you to come or to stay with them?

You can visit Castle McCulloch, shown here, in Jamestown where gold was mined years ago. This story is two folktales blended into one because in Oak Ridge, on Highway 68 in another part of the county, is the Old Mill. It is a beautiful place to visit and experience the bygone days when mills grinded wheat. Linger awhile and you can picture the stories I've told. They have fine bags of flour and grits. Another restored old water mill in the Piedmont is Murray's Mill out near Newton and Hickory. One of the few remaining covered bridges is near there too, so you can visit both for a feeling of these folktales. *Photo by Theresa Bane.*

Chapter Five:

Lexington

The Barbecue Capitol of the World

The first settlers, Germans, came to the area in the 1750s to have religious freedom. It was first known as "The Dutch Settlement on Abbotts Creek" or "The Settlement on Abbotts Creek." Valentine Leonard, a hero of the Battle of Guilford County Courthouse, was one of the founding fathers. The settlers prospered, building a community and a mill to serve the area. The Leonard family, along with the other settlers, established the first Pilgrim Church and graveyard, both of which are still in use today.

As time passed and more and more settlers came into the area, the name of the town changed from Abbotts Creek to Lexington in honor of Lexington, Massachusetts, the location of the first skirmish of the American Revolutionary War. In 1828, it was incorporated into a city and made the county seat. Throughout its history the town has always thrived, relying on the revenue of its textile mills. Unfortunately, in the 1990s, the mills began to close and relocate out of the country, taking both their jobs and money with them.

Today, Lexington is known for its famous barbecue and has been host to one of the state's largest outdoor street festival since 1984. Pork-shoulder that has been cooked slowly over a hardwood fire and served with vinegar based sauce and red-slaw on the side is what Lexington-style barbecue is all about.

The Hero, Valentine Leonard

If you come by for Sunday dinner at the Browns' house, you'll get good Southern home cookin' and you'll hear everyone call my husband, Fred, by the name "Leonard." Nowadays everyone else calls him Fred and has for, oh, almost forty years, but at home he is "Leonard." Leonard is his mama's, or as Fred says, "Mother's," maiden name. She grew up around there with her daddy, Joe Leonard. He was in charge of the town water plant on Abbotts Creek.

A log cabin in Lexington. *Photo by Cynthia.*

Pilgrim Church graveyard dates back to the 1700s. The large memorial you see here was erected to commemorate the two murdered heroes, Valentine Leonard and Wooldrich Fritz who gave their lives for freedom. *Photo by Fred Brown.*

I knew that Lexington, North Carolina, was famous for its barbecue and was very historic. I'd even been to Lexington over the years, but thanks to family storytelling, I heard about the 250-year-old Pilgrim Church graveyard and the present-day Pilgrim Church, the fourth such worship structure on the 250-year-old site. One of its primary founding families was, yes, the historic Leonard family.

One Sunday after dinner, Jeff, Fred's sister's Patricia's husband, mentioned Valentine Leonard as we were discussing this book. Jeff and Patricia were married, as were Mother and Dad, at Pilgrim Church. They all visit Lexington and the old graveyard there frequently. Jeff said, "Let me tell you the story. Valentine Leonard was a hero of the Revolutionary War. Why, he even fought at the Battle of Guilford Court House with General Nathanael Greene. His story is interesting. You gotta look at 'the book'."

I was intrigued and began doing research. By now even Fred (Leonard) was interested and helping. Thanks to Pat, Jeff, Mother, and Dad, they had copies for us to use of "the book," commonly known as *The Dutch Settlement at Abbotts Creek*. It was written years ago by the church's former pastor, the Reverend J. Everette Neese. He wrote that the Leonards were among the early German immigrants that came down from Pennsylvania in the 1740s to settle on the bountiful, rich farmland around Abbott's Creek; it's now known as Lexington. They built houses, laid claim to hundreds of acres, and began farming with a peaceful life communing with nature. Naturally, a church would be an important part of their life.

Pilgrim Church and graveyard, according to the historians, began around 1753 or 1754 as an open brush arbor. Later sanctuaries were each bigger and better all the way to present day 2010. That's 250 years! The graveyard is famous in its own right because of the intricate carvings in soapstone by the German woodworkers who came to settle. According to local historians, they are unique in America and include the "pierced" designs that are cutouts in the stone — all this here in the Piedmont of North Carolina! Even during our frequent trips to Germany, Fred and I didn't see this many pierced headstones in one graveyard. One of the founders of the church and settlement was their family's most famous ancestor: Valentine Leonard.

When Valentine laid eyes on Elizabeth, he fell in love. Valentine Leonard was a tall, rugged, and handsome German man. His family had immigrated to Pennsylvania from far away Germany in Europe to a new beginning and religious freedom in America. He'd lived only a short while in his new homeland of America. His trade of tailoring was good work. But he longed for adventure, even more to explore his new country. Elizabeth felt the same way, so Valentine was delighted when she agreed to marry him and leave for the new land to the south.

Travel was hard in those days and, one evening along the way, Valentine talked by the campfire. "I just did not know that the way was rough and the trip so hard. I am sorry, my dear. But soon we will be able to rest and begin our new life." Valentine brushed Elizabeth's hair away from her tired but lovely face as he talked quietly.

Elizabeth smiled. "I am not complaining, my husband, I am merely eager to see this godly land you tell us about." It had been a long journey of two weeks by wagon from Pennsylvania for the settlers. Everyone was ready for it to be finished. Then, at last, they were there.

They'd heard that what is now known as the Piedmont, North Carolina, was a bountiful land for farming, raising cattle, and peaceful living. The beautiful rolling hills and sparkling rivers and creeks in endless forests reminded them of their homeland in Germany. Yes, it was indeed idyllic from their first glimpse. After a short rest, they began their new life. They worked together to do the building. Valentine and his wife chose a perfect home site between Abbotts Creek and Mill Creek.

"This is so beautiful, Valentine. I'd like you to build us a strong house that will weather what the years bring," said Elizabeth. They planned together with drawings and laughter. Valentine planned a large mansion for his pretty wife Elizabeth. Trees were cut, fields cleared, the labor was hard, day after day, dawn to dusk. But the satisfaction of doing it for their future kept the men, women, and children going.

Slowly but surely the houses were finished. They were tireless, hardworking pioneers. Life was so full of work, friends, and the land. Valentine and Elizabeth flourished. They had always wanted a large happy family. So their five strapping sons and three sweet daughters were such a blessing in their happy home. Normal life settled in. Valentine and Elizabeth enjoyed their family and neighbors. They built their gristmill on Mill Creek, which they began calling "Leonhardts Creek" from the original German of Leonard. It served much of the growing settlement around.

Building Their Church

One of the first community projects was a meetinghouse for a church. Religious freedom was one of their reasons for coming to America, so the construction and location of the new church was a top priority.

On a sunny afternoon Valentine was out riding with some of his men. They stopped in a peaceful grove of trees to rest the horses. "Wait, look at this right here. It is so peaceful in this grove... This is where we build our house of the Lord." Valentine smiled broadly as he told the group. They had found the idyllic setting for their Pilgrim Church. He and his fellow settlers loved their church and were dedicated to it.

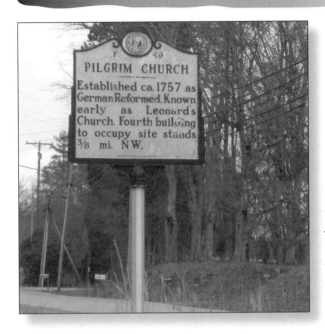

PILGRIM CHURCH

Established ca. 1757 as German Reformed. Known early as Leonard's Church. Fourth building to occupy site stands ⅜ mi. N W.

Reverend J. Everette Neese's book *Dutch Settlement at Abbotts Creek* is an excellent resource for the history of Pilgrim Church as well as Valentine Leonard. *Photo by Fred Brown.*

The first structure would be very simple. A brush arbor, a simple structure made of just small tree branches, would be enough for their church services at first. "We will worship in our native German language to honor our heritage," Valentine said as he made a broad gesture. They did worship in their new rustic retreat embracing the religious freedom in their new homeland. Soon a simple structure would replace it and a church building was erected. As was the custom, the graveyard was begun beside the church, but it was special. The skilled woodcarvers from Germany who had settled at Abbotts Creek carved intricate, artistic gravestones. Many had the style of piercing the stone in designs that were unique. Valentine and Elizabeth took such pride in their church. They hoped it would found a heritage for centuries to come.

Life went on at Abbotts Creek. Valentine and his family continued to prosper with hard work and devotion to the land they loved as well as to each other. Their new homeland of America was the best place to be.

The years seemed to slip by quickly. As they sat by the fire one evening, Valentine and Elizabeth talked quietly. She said, "Valentine, you're now such a great man. Everyone looks to you for important matters. The years have gone so fast and I am so proud of you. Yet I worry about the news we continue to hear that America is heading for war with the British. What will they ask of you? You are past the age of serving in the army. Whatever is going to happen?"

Truth be known, Valentine had been thinking and worrying about the same thing himself. Not wanting to alarm his wife though, Valentine reassured her. "Now, now, we aren't even sure this will happen, my dear. No need to worry. Let us wait to see what the future holds."

The news became grimmer with each passing day until it seemed that war was inevitable. Alas, trouble did come as the young nation declared its independence from Great Britain. War was declared, and the battles began. Valentine was a fiercely loyal American. He preached that to the other settlers. He felt he had to enlist in the army to help defend their country's freedom. Valentine loved his adopted homeland so much that he came to a fateful decision. Although he was a powerful, wealthy man already fifty-five years old, he joined the army to help fight the Revolutionary War with England. His five sons eventually followed their father so all were there at the Battle of Guilford Court House.

Elizabeth was heartbroken. She tearfully hugged and kissed them goodbye, hoping and praying that her men would come home safely. The men rode off; Valentine and his friend, Wooldrich Fritz, led the way on that sunny morning. It was with a heavy heart that Elizabeth, her daughters, and the other families waited at home. Most of the Piedmont families chose to help in America's fight. In fact, Valentine had encouraged the rebellion. He used his position and standing in the community to influence his neighbors. Because of this he was hated by the Tories among his neighbors. Of course there were small pockets of those fearful of change and still loyal to the British. Some of these Tories in the area tried their best to fight the rising tide of America's cause.

News of the battles came sporadically to the Pilgrim Church settlement, and Elizabeth waited and watched impatiently, day-by-day, for letters or news of her returning men. It was shocking when they heard that the British were nearby in Guilford County. The families were fearful as the news spread like wildfire. The brave men and their sons fought hard with General Nathanael Greene at Guilford Court House to stop the powerful General Cornwallis and his bigger and better equipped English army. That battle was one of the turning points of the Revolutionary War. General Greene and his men would go down in history, as would the events that happened at Guilford County Courthouse on Thursday, March 15, 1781.

You can imagine the joyful homecoming of Valentine Leonard and all five of his sons. Why, there was celebrating and festivities for days. After everything settled down, after rest for their bodies and souls, the men returned to the daily work of the hundreds of acres of Leonard land. Elizabeth was so happy to have them home again. Each day was a bright one. The war was nearing an end. Yet still the Tories were strong in their beliefs that the British should be victorious instead of the Americans. They made it no secret that they hated Valentine, especially because he was a powerful supporter of the revolution that many in the area followed.

It was a few short months, but the terrible war memories and nightmares were fading day by day. Elizabeth and the girls had prepared an especially fine dinner that the whole family enjoyed. The fall weather was beginning to turn cooler, but Elizabeth and her beloved husband sat comfortably by the big, eight-foot-long fireplace hearth with the top of their large front doors open. They rested and talked quietly as dusk fell. The sun had set and twilight was upon them.

"I am weary, but it feels so good in my bones and in my soul to once again work our land." Valentine smiled as he caressed Elizabeth's hand.

"My heart is bursting with pride and love for you, dear, dear husband of mine," Elizabeth said as she hugged him, then rose to get a last cup of tea for both of them.

So intent with each other, neither of them saw a quick movement at the door. When the savage shots rang out, they brutally struck the Patriot Valentine. He fell to the floor mortally wounded as Elizabeth's seemingly endless screams echoed through the suddenly silent and dark house. The cowardly Tory assassins escaped to go on to the home of Fritz Wooldrich, where they shot him dead too. The critically wounded Valentine lay near death for eleven days, before finally succumbing to the Tories' acid hatred-fueled murderous shots.

Valentine Leonard and Fritz Wooldrich, the two Patriots, were buried side by side in the Pilgrim Church cemetery, the church that Valentine had helped to establish on the land he donated. Special carved soapstone tombstones marked their final resting place.

In 1896, a tall, beautiful white marble monument was erected to honor the two men. One of the inscriptions reads: "The heroes buried in this spot were cruelly assassinated in their own home by Tories near the close of the Revolutionary War. They were Patriots and bravely fought for American independence." Today that monument and many unique German gravestones are next to the modern Pilgrim Church. The spirits linger along with the memory of departed loved ones, whose lives touch us from beyond the grave.

Valentine will be remembered as a hero of the Battle of Guilford Court House hopefully for centuries to come. If you walk in the quiet amongst the ancient graves, you may have a feeling that his spirit still lingers in the lands he loved. The tall, beautiful white marble monument to honor Valentine and his friend Fritz Wooldrich graces the graveyard and reminds all of the brave men who fought for the freedom we enjoy today.

This plate, distributed by I. C. Griffin of Concord, North Carolina, depicts the former Pilgrim Evangelical and Reformed Church structure. It is from the collection of Pat and Jeff Manuel. The reverse side reads:

> In 1753 or 1754, German settlers selected the site for Pilgrim (Leonard's) Reformed Church as one "fashioned by god for a house of Worship." The chosen site was on an unoccupied tract of 50 acres of the Lord Granville lands near the stream known as Leonard's Creek. For some time services were conducted under a brush arbor. The first church, built during 1757-1764, was of logs with a gallery on three sides and a tall goblet pulpit at the front. In 1783, a "Letters Patent" was secured from the state of North Carolina designating the tract as church property "forever." Records show infant baptisms dating from 1757. The earliest marked grave is 1761. The log church was used until 1807, and was by then a union church, being used by Reformed and Lutheran congregations. Together they built a frame structure arranged very much like the first. In 1882, a third and larger building was dedicated. In 1903 there was a division of property, with the Reformed group buying the larger tract of land and the house of worship. An educational building was added at the rear of the church in 1935. In 1951, this addition was further enlarged and the sanctuary renovated."

The Spirits of Abbotts Creek

The balmy summer breeze fluttered the leaves above the creek. The heat of the night felt heavy. Luther and Buddy had been best friends since they were little. Their favorite thing to do on summer nights was to take a lantern to hunt possums in the woods near home on Abbotts Creek. Most of the time they just laughed and joked as they tromped around in the dark. Sometimes, they got lucky and they came home with a little somethin' for their mamas to cook for supper.

This evening, however, they had been hunting for what seemed like hours. They hadn't gotten one, not even a glimpse of a critter, or even a pair of red eyes. They both were hot and tired. It was Luther's idea to go swimming in the cool dark water of Abbotts Creek. It looked so nice and peaceful; you could hear the Southern night sounds of crickets or katydid song and see the tiny glow of lightning bugs flitting here and there.

Luther and Buddy were laughing, having fun, splashing, and talkin', when suddenly a loud sound up on the hill startled them. Before they could get out of the water to investigate, they saw what looked like a flaming wooden barrel come rolling and crashing down through the woods toward them. They watched with terrified eyes as the barrel came right down to the water's edge, but what happened next was even stranger. They heard a splash as the flaming barrel crashed into the water, but there was not so much as a single ripple on the surface of the creek where the barrel went into the water.

Photo by Cynthia.

"What in tarnation was that?" Luther yelled. Screaming with panic, the friends scrambled out of the creek, grabbed their clothes, and hightailed it outta there. They didn't stop a-runnin' till they got all the way up to Pilgrim Church Road.

Breathin' hard, they were still shakin' with fear when they finally stopped. They struggled into their damp, dirty clothes just as a few old fellas rode up in their wagons. They'd heard all the hollering Luther and Buddy had done and came to see what the ruckus was all about.

Luther and Buddy were mighty happy to see that help arrived. They told the group about the flaming barrel coming outta nowhere rolling down the hill and into the creek. At first no one believed them. In fact, they began laughing at them. However, the hilarity died down as everyone saw bright orbs of light appearing in the woods next to the road. It seemed as if the orbs were floating and moving slowly around like lantern light, but without someone there holding a lantern — no one alive and breathin', that is.

One of the men said, "We better get outta here fast! Come on, Luther, you and Buddy can ride in the wagon with me." The group scattered quickly, heading toward home with Luther and Buddy riding in their new friend's wagon as fast as they could make it go.

Fact or Legend

As you can imagine, everyone was talking about it all week long. No one could explain the odd occurrences. Sure enough, the next time someone was walking in the woods after dark, the same mysterious orbs appeared and then disappeared. It was also said that several times some of the fellas who had been out with their dogs hunting at night had spooky things happen to them. All of a sudden their dogs went wild chasing after something. Trouble was none of them could see anything and the dogs kept circling and running back around the same area like after some ghost or phantom.

Legend has it that when General Cornwallis left the Battle of Guilford Court House in Greensboro, he traveled through those woods. His war-torn men struggled to keep up the pace. It was known that Cornwallis had stolen gold, silver coins, and other such spoils of war in his sweep across North Carolina. They were dragging these bags and barrels full of it as they rushed out of the area. Yet, they also had to carry their food and other provisions they needed that was very important to the army. The tired horses and soldiers were exhausted.

The legend goes on to say that when Cornwallis and his men got to Abbotts Creek, the general ordered some of his men to cut loose one of the barrels, letting it roll into the creek. Probably he planned to double back to reclaim the treasure later. This would make a lighter load on the

The headstone reads "Site of Brush Arbor and first house of worship Pilgrim Reformed Church CA 1753-1757." Photo by Fred Brown

horses so they could move faster. When the barrel rolled down, it crashed into a deep part of Abbotts Creek, forever disappearing from sight. The unlucky army had unknowingly picked one of the deepest parts of the creek, as it was more of a river back then with very deep places. So the story goes that Cornwallis had to abandon his ill-gotten goods. He never got back to reclaim his stolen gold.

Some of these strange stories and more have been told and retold about the ghosts of Abbotts Creek for years. Folks would see the orbs of light floating in the woods like a large group of men with lanterns walking around, but there was no group of people — just empty, lonely woods.

Another story was told over and over about loud voices and sounds around the creek and its nearby woods when no one was there. Over the years there have been many others who encountered strange, spooky happenings in the woods around Abbotts Creek near Pilgrim Church.

So don't go alone. When the sun goes down, and the night sounds are the only thing you hear in those woods, that's when it could happen. You too might see some of the spirits of Abbotts Creek. Just remember one chilling thought: General Cornwallis never got back to reclaim his gold.

Well, at least when he was living and breathing, that is.

Chapter Six:

Old Salem

Old Salem is an historic district in the city of Winston-Salem, North Carolina; it's located between Race Street, Old Salem Road, Horse Street, and Brookstone Avenue. The district also includes the buildings along the east side of Church Street and some parts of a Moravian cemetery known as God's Acre. Old Salem was declared a national landmark in 1966.

Originally settled by Moravians, a Protestant denomination, Salem was to be the center town of a 98,000-acre tract of land once known as Wachovia. Construction began in 1766 to build the administrative, economic, and religious centers. Salem was controlled by the church that owned the land and leased it out. Everyone who lived in the community had to be a member of the church and remain in good standing. To leave or to be asked to leave the church also meant that you had to leave Salem as well.

In 1849, Salem refused to be the county seat for Forsyth County, a responsibility that went to the town of Winston, which soon became a thriving industrial center. Nearly ten years later the church allowed the residents of the town to buy their property, allowing it to become a legal municipality.

Winston and Salem merged together in 1913, becoming the first and only community to be an officially hyphenated name for a United States Post Office. In the 1950s, Old Salem, Inc., a non-profit organization, was developed to save and restore the historic buildings of the area that is now known as Old Salem. It succeeded and now operates many of the buildings as museums, living museums, period restaurants, and gift shops.

The Little Red Man

The Moravians settled in the area that is now known as Winston-Salem, North Carolina. Nowadays you can visit the charmingly restored village called Old Salem. It's a grand place with its restored buildings you can go in them and visit the houses where the Moravians actually lived and worked. They were the hardworking German descendants of many of the people who live there today, and it was said that they worked even long past the sun had set for the day. It feels as if you have gone back in time. The village also has a working bakery that bakes all those Moravian sugar cake recipes and the thin Moravian cookies that everyone loves so very much, so while visiting the buildings there, you can smell the sugar cakes and hear the stories.

Back then, all the single young men lived in what is known as The Single Brother's House. This crowd of young men had a good time living together and enjoyed each other's company. At night, after the supper dishes were cleaned and put away, they would all sit around the fire in the main room telling stories to one another. Some of the men who lived there were especially hardworking. After dinner was eaten and the mess cleaned, they were ready to keep right on working. These men would go down to the cellar and pick up where the others had left off. You see, the brothers were enlarging their house because they had more brothers living there than they really had room for and more single men were arriving all the time. To accommodate the men, they had to make room for the ones to come, so they were digging out space in the cellar to make a whole new room.

It took a lot of teamwork to get the job done. They would dig out buckets of dirt and then those would need to be taken outside and dumped. It was hard to get back underneath in some places as they were digging into the darkest and deepest part of the cellar. That's where Little Red came in. This brother got his nickname because he always wore a red hat and he was very, very short — shorter than anyone else there. He didn't like to say it, but he was even shorter than some of the ladies. Nevertheless, he was a cheerful guy, always whistling a tune or telling funny stories. Because he was small he was perfect for getting up under and getting that dirt out so that the bigger guys could carry it on out, but one night a tragedy happened. As our Little Red Man was digging, all of a sudden the earth gave way and came crashing down

The Single Brother's House in Old Salem, Winston-Salem, North Carolina. Does the Little Red Man still haunt it? *Photo by Cynthia.*

on top of our friend. Frantically, the others tried to dig out the dirt that had fallen down on their friend, but by the time they were able to reach him, it was too late.

The loss of the Little Red Man was felt by all of his friends. They missed him dearly and they would talk about him at supper, about what a cheerful gentleman he was. They remembered fondly all the jokes he told and how he loved to whistle. Also, the work was much harder without him too.

One night as one of the brothers was going down to the cellar to work, he felt somebody push him on his shoulder. He whirled around to find out who was bothering him and — nobody was there. He went back upstairs quickly and demanded to know who had been down there pushing on him and everybody looked at him in a strange blank way. They had all been upstairs.

Everyone kind of brushed it off and forgot about it, but the next night two brothers were down there in the cellar trying to get a little work done and they heard whistling. One of them said, "Why, that sounds just like our friend the Little Red Man." He whirled around quickly to see who could have been doing it, but as soon as he did, the whistling stopped. The two brothers were all alone in the lantern-lit cellar.

Strange happenings like this continued on throughout the construction of the new room. At first the brothers who lived there were afraid of these mysterious happenings, but then it occurred to them that this was their friend, Little Red Man, and they found a kind of comfort in the fact that he was still there with them, even if only in spirit. From then on the brothers looked forward to those times when they would hear just a few notes of his whistle. Or when they would get the feeling that someone was there with them, even if when they would whirl around and nobody would be there.

The legend of the Little Red Man haunting The Single Brother's House continues on to this day. If you ever go and visit Old Salem, they'll show you where the single men lived and worked and maybe, just maybe they will even tell you the story if you ask them. No one has seen the Little Red Man lately. Perhaps he's finally resting in peace now that modern times have come, but if you should be outside walking by The Single Brother's House and hear a mysterious whistle, you'll know who it is and that the Little Red Man is still there, just visiting with his friends.

Chapter Seven:
Siler City

Balanced for Progress

First settled during the 1750s as a farming and railway town in Chatham County, Siler City is the home of Jordan Lake, a popular boating, camping, and fishing attraction, but it may best be known as "that place" just outside of the fictional town Mayberry, North Carolina from the 1960s television comedy "The Andy Griffith Show."

Siler City was originally a railroad depot that opened up in 1884, located between Greensboro and Sanford, North Carolina. It was named after Samuel Siler, who donated the land. The railroad encouraged the area to grow, as it developed almost a dozen stores, three livery stables, three hotels, tobacco warehouses, a cotton gin, and sawmill. It also had the distinction of being the largest shipping point for rabbits in the country. Siler City was incorporated in 1887.

Beginning in 1900 and booming onward, the town made record growth and expanded, adding streetlights, telephone lines, water and sewer systems, town offices, a mayor, and a jail — all by 1927. Industrial plants began to move into the area and locally-owned and operated businesses did well. The population increased steadily until 1980 and then began to fall off. Today between 8,000 and 10,000 people call Siler City home.

Devil's Tramping Ground

Back in the 1950s and '60s there were still lots of wonderful forests in North Carolina. One of our family favorite Saturday outings was to go exploring in the endless beautiful "woods." My brother Mack and I were both in the Scouts, so we loved nature and the "hikes" our Daddy took us on. Even back then I wasn't much of a hiker and got tired fast. Mack can tell you the funny story of how I'd lie down on the soft pine needles in the middle of the trail, pleading to "just rest" a short time while he and Daddy laughed. It's still a family joke, but Mack, our younger brother Brad, and I continue to respect nature and enjoy the woods because of

Photo by Cynthia.

those wonderful Saturdays. The Devil's Tramping Ground story reminds me of our hikes. It is also a real favorite when I tell stories to Scouts.

Back in the day before computers, television, and video games took up too much time, kids spent more time outside playing and enjoying nature and most days after school that's what the two friends would do as soon as they got home. On free Saturdays they were allowed to go on hikes and camp near home in the vast pine forests. One sunny day such as this, the two boys set off with their packs to explore. They walked and talked, stopping only for some water from their canteens. This Saturday they wanted to go someplace new so they searched for a new camping spot. The sun disappeared, making the forest darker as they came to a

clearing. It was strange looking, that circular area. Not a single leaf, stick, or pine needle lay in the clearing. It was blackened, charred-looking bare earth. Intrigued by the oddness, the boys decided this would be a good camping place. They began to set up their tent and build a fire. However, when they lit the campfire the flames blazed so high that both boys jumped back in fright. The fire seemed to get larger in spite of their efforts to put out the edges. When they were finally able to extinguish it, the boys were too shaken to stay. Grabbing their gear, they rushed through the darkened forest fast to get home.

Things didn't seem so scary the next day when they told the story, so when they realized they had forgotten some of their things, they went back to get them with their dads to find the clearing. They found it, but were shocked to see that the circle was even more trampled and blackened. Every trace of their camp was gone and they found their things lying beyond in the trees. It was very strange indeed.

Over the years many have visited the same circular barren earth. Biologists have done tests, and foresters tried to plant new trees. Always, the next day everything is outside the circle and the earth the same. Some have dared to spend the night nearby so they could watch all night. No one ever lasted all night — before dawn they'd come running out telling tales of horrible noises, weird lights, and even the sound of a horse.

The clearing is there in that forest, waiting for you. See if you encounter anything strange, but … *don't* visit alone.

Chapter Eight:
Summerfield

Respectful of the Past; Focused on the Future

FAMILY CEMETERY OF
CHARLES BRUCE
——1733-1832——
Revolutionary Leader
and Founder of Bruce's Cross Roads
(now Summerfield)
and
grave of James Gillies
Light Horse Harry Lee's Bugler
slain by British Feb. 12, 1781.

Founded in 1769 by the American Revolutionary patriot, Charles Bruce, the community was named Bruce's Crossroads. The town changed its name to Summerfield in 1812 with the opening of its new post office to honor the evangelist John Summerfield (1798-1825).

Located in Guilford County, Summerfield has both rolling woods and open countryside, making it a popular place to live. The town incorporated in 1998 to avoid being annexed by the city of Greensboro. Summerfield, with its population still less than 10,000 people, is known for having excellent schools and being a great place to raise a family. In recent years, archeologists have found arrowheads among the chipping grounds, proving that Summerfield was populated by humans for thousands of years prior to its founding.

The Apple Tree

When we moved into our new house on Pleasant Ridge Road, Greensboro had not yet come all the way out to where we were. We called it "the country," and it was country back then, as there were only farms and livestock around. It was said that our plot of land had been a strawberry field and I had no trouble believing it. The soil was terrible: it had lots of stones and a body just had to work really hard to get anything to grow there. We never found any arrowheads, but then again, we never plowed. There was nothing on our patch of land.

If you were to visit my home now, you wouldn't even recognize it. After better than thirty years, we and the birds have planted trees, bushes, and flowers, lots of flowers. It's a green and lush place now. But back when we moved in, the only thing that was growing on my homestead was way out in the back of the property, and it was an old and twisted

Photo by Cynthia.

The waterfall on Old Oak Ridge Road, Summerfield, North Carolina. *Photo by Cynthia.*

and gnarled apple tree. This tree looked like it had been there for years and years and years. I figured a tree that old would have some good apples and I waited anxiously for them to grow and ripen. But when it came time, the apples were really small and brown and fit only for the families of deer and rabbits. They seemed to like the apples just fine, and to this day those animals return and eat the apples fallen from that old and gnarled tree in the back of my yard. That tree back there reminds me of the tree in this story…

The plantation antebellum mansion was big and beautiful, giving you the idea that the family that was living there was living a "happily ever after" life. The man of the house lived there with his Aunt Sally, his wife, and their two children. He was a tall man and an upstanding citizen to boot, so when the Civil War broke out, it was no surprise that he joined up, becoming an officer.

With the war begun, folks just didn't believe that it was ever going to come as far south as Greensboro, North Carolina, or even into the South at all, let alone right near their very own home. But as the war spread and the battles increased, the father began to worry about his family.

Finally he said, "I've got to go away now to fight in the war. I want somebody here to protect you."

"We'll be fine," Old Aunt Sally said. "We are strong women, but it wouldn't hurt to have the children protected."

The children were sent far across the ocean to England to stay with family there until after the war was over. Good thing too, as the war was much worse than anyone thought. It was a horrible time and yes indeed, just like so many other homes, theirs was burned. The pretty young wife was taken with a fever soon after. Only Aunt Sally survived. Her favorite apple tree in the backyard and a small barn were all that was left. She lived in the barn and took care of those who were left. Her nephew never returned from the war. Old Aunt Sally managed as best as she could. She was old and passed away before the children could return home after the war from their stay in England. In fact, they were still overseas when she died.

No one can really pinpoint when it all started except to say it was after the war had ended. It was probably noticed by one of the local boys out walking with his dog along the road. As it got later and later and darker and darker, he hurried on along because he didn't want to get in trouble with his mama. That's when he saw it — a fog-like white shape on the side of the road. The road was really just an old rambling path that wandered through the woods, a shortcut to his home. When he saw that patch of creepy, floating white fog, a fear touched his heart. Faster and faster he walked and the fog kept pace with him, maybe even catching up. He walked faster and faster until he was running and still the fog lingered.

When he got home, nobody would believe him of course, but it wasn't long before other people started to have the same strange experience. It was near where the old gnarled apple tree and the mansion ruins still loomed. They would see and hear strange things. Why, this one time, one of the neighbor ladies was out there picking blackberries at dusk and she swore that she saw somebody made of that creepy fog standing right there by the tree. It looked like a woman, wild looking, in a smoky white gown and flowing white hair that was streaming and blowing in a wind. Even the sight of the apple tree frightened her, looking more like skeletal hands sticking up out of the ground ready to grab at you or anything else. Some folks began to speculate that maybe it was a ghost, maybe it was Aunt Sally, but why would she be haunting the land? The story began to spread and soon everybody had heard it. More and more folks began to see the ghost. Well, I don't have to tell you that people were careful not to go out there unless they really had to, especially at night.

By and by the years rolled on and the burnt-out house got even more ruined looking. The grass grew up tall all around it, the windows were broken out, even the porch had fallen off, but wouldn't you know it — the old apple tree that looked like a skeletal hand was still standing there. It was as old as ever and all twisted, but it stood there like it was guarding the house. Stories about whatever it was that folks were seeing and hearing out that way continued on over the years. Every now and again somebody would get good and scared by what they saw, somebody or something ready to jump out and grab them. All this time the apple tree stood, letting its small brown apples fall to feed the deer and rabbits that seemed to enjoy them.

With the war over and time passed, the children finally came home. The daughter had grown into a lovely young lady, firm and strong. She had long ago made up her mind that she was going to restore her family home to the glory it once was, but when she finally got there and saw the place, the reality set in. She knew that it would be no easy task and was going to take a long time and a lot more money and resources than she was going to be able to gather together on her own. She certainly didn't intend to marry just to have a husband who would pay for it. She decided that she was still going to do it by herself, but that it was just going to take time. She had some of the lumber cut and had enough money to have a little house built for herself. When trying to decide exactly where to put it, she thought about it and finally said, "You know, I can remember back to a long, long time ago that my Aunt Sally loved that old apple tree. I can remember us sitting under it and her telling me stories and eating apples. They were nice and sweet and good back then so I think that would be the best place for the house."

Photo by Cynthia.

The day of the ground-breaking was simply beautiful — bright and sunny. Nothing unusual or scary had happened in the area for awhile now so even some of the neighbors turned out for the event. Oh, it was such a joyous occasion; the daughter was well received by society and everyone liked her so much. When the workman took his shovel and dug it deep into the ground, the girl could just feel her heart soaring. She was going to have a small place to live true, but she was going to work hard on bringing back her family name. She didn't know how long it would take but she was determined that she was going to keep trying no matter what.

The workman toiled at their job, digging deeper and deeper, and then everybody there heard it — a loud CLANK! Every person there froze and turned to look at the workman who had just about broke his shovel against whatever hard thing was buried in the ground. They all gathered close as they watched him push the dirt aside and did a little more digging. Much to their surprise, the workman pulled up a small iron box with a huge lock on it.

There was a great deal of excitement about it and everyone wanted to break the lock off and see what was inside. Of course the young daughter gave her permission for them to do so right away, so the workman broke the lock off and opened up the little iron chest. Inside was an old bag and some papers. They took out the old bag, but it was so old that as they did so it fell apart. Tumbling down into their hands were emeralds! Emerald rings, emerald necklaces, emerald bracelets, emerald earrings… Oh my gracious, there were emeralds! Nothing had ever gleamed and glittered as beautiful in the sun as those emeralds did.

"Why, these belonged to my Aunt Sally!" the daughter said as soon as she saw the jewelry. "These pieces of jewelry were just believed to have been lost all these years, back during the war, maybe when the house burned down. How did they get under the apple tree? Who put them there?"

That night the daughter sat in a rocking chair in front of a little fire. She was rocking back and forth, thinking about the emeralds. She had since put them in a safe place, I can assure you of that. As she sat there rocking, all she could think about was her Aunt Sally and how she had to have been the one who hid the jewels. A lot of people did this during the war to hide their precious things and that must have been what old Aunt Sally did, but she died before she could tell her family. That explained why that spirit was haunting the area. The daughter knew — *just knew* — that it had to be the spirit of her aunt that was the misty gray fog who was guarding the jewels all these years, faithfully scaring off the wrong people while trying to entice the right one to stay.

After the daughter recovered the family jewels, there were no more sightings of the foggy gray mist taking on a ghostly shape near the gnarled old apple tree. The jewels had been discovered! With the money she would be able to restore the family's home and name to what it once was. Finally Aunt Sally could rest in peace.

Bruce's Crossroads

When we moved into our new house on Pleasant Ridge Road, we discovered that it had been built atop what used to be a strawberry field. All the way around and surrounding us was nothing but fields of bad ground and one old, craggily, scraggly apple tree that managed to grow at the back of our property. I tried my hardest to have a garden out there, but the only thing I was ever able to coax out of the ground was one measly little watermelon and deer got to it.

I was able, however, to get my husband, Fred, to dig holes for me to plant trees. I got trees from my grandmother and mother. I got trees from Fred's grandmother and his mother. I even got trees from the state of North Carolina Forestry, thank you very much. Fred dug hole after hole and I planted tree after tree. I wanted to plant a row of white pines like a column of guards because the fella who owned the lot behind us kept plowing and plowing up his field and getting closer and closer to our property. I figured it was just a matter of time until he came over the line, even if accidentally. "Honey," I said to Fred, "we need to get something to grow real fast out there, like some nice white pines."

The Charles Bruce and Jamie Gillis memorial sits outside Summerfield School, Pleasant Ridge, North Carolina. Gillis was the beloved bugler boy of Revolutionary War Colonel Light Horse Henry Lee. *Photo by Theresa Bane.*

I took on the project myself and set out to get me four of the nicest and strongest-looking white pines. Back then there was a really nice family that had a landscaping business close to town, near Lake Higgins on this side of Highway 220 North, what is now the Brassfield Shopping Center. I went there a lot and liked the folks who ran it. It was where I got all my gardening supplies and it was where I went to get my trees as well.

I explained to the fella who ran it what I wanted and he said it wouldn't be a problem at all to get me the trees, but I said to him, "Now these are kind of big. Do you think you can come out and kind of plant them?" He nodded his head and said yeah sure, he could come over to my place; I only had to pay him a small sum of money.

The day he came out to my place to plant those trees for me was a kind of a gray day. It wasn't raining mind you, just one of those damp fall days. As they were digging the holes, I was talking to the fella, chit-chattering away like I always do and asking him all kinds of questions about trees and stuff when he looks up and over to me and says, "Have you seen anything peculiar 'round here?"

I got quiet for a moment and then said, "What do you mean by 'peculiar?'"

He said to me, "Well, this part of the county is so old and historic. There's a folktale about the Bugler Boy who was killed by the Red Coats during the Revolutionary War. Have you seen the ghost of the bugle boy?"

Again I was quiet for a moment before I spoke. "Uh, no, sir."

He then told me this true story of the little Bugler Boy of Bruce's Crossroads…

Long and ago the town of Summerfield used to be called Bruce's Crossroads. At that time you could see the Revolutionary War Colonel Light Horse Henry Lee marching his troops back and forth in regiment as he got them ready for war. You see, these volunteers were going off to save Guilford County from the British. Like all troops, they had themselves a bugler boy and theirs was named Jamie Gillis. Oh, I reckon he was maybe just a teenager himself but his bugle was the very sound and call for all. When Jamie let loose with "toot, toot, toot, toot, toot!" everybody knew that it was time to rally the men and get ready to march. Henry Lee's bugle boy was well loved by his compatriots, especially by the older gentlemen in the troop. They believed Jamie to be the nicest young man they had ever met.

Well, eventually the war did come to Guilford County and you can read all about it in your history books. I suppose what's important to know is that the British came here for battle. One of the single most important battles of the whole Revolutionary War was fought right here in Guilford County. Light Horse Henry Lee and his men were there, bugler boy and all.

There was the firing of cannons and the air filled with shot and a whole long wicked battle was fought, but when the smoke cleared at the end of the day, Guilford County was safe. The battle had been lost to the British but losing it would enable us to win the war. Just nobody realized it yet.

Lee's troops made their way back toward their homes, straggling, all tired and worn and beaten. As wounded as they were, they were thinking about all those who had just died; they had to be heart sickened by the whole thing.

As the story goes, Lee's bugle boy was walking back home through the woods that day, leading his gray pony as he went. That's when it happened!

Some of those British were having a party I guess, soaking up their glory and telling everybody who'd listen how they won the battle. Truth of it is, those British soldiers were supposed to be hightailing it up Horse Pen Creek and leaving the area but these few men didn't. They had been having their own little party and things were getting out of hand. It was dusk and they weren't being careful or paying attention to what they were doing. Suddenly one of the soldiers saw an enemy uniform in the gathering darkness. They started shooting off their guns. The soldiers couldn't see in the darkness that he was such a young man. One of those bullets hit and killed poor, sweet Jamie. He fell dead to the ground, his bugle hitting the ground right next to him.

It was such a senseless thing, Jamie's death, especially after he had fought so hard at the Battle of Guilford Court House. The bugle boy was mourned and deeply missed by everyone who knew him. He was never forgotten and is to this day honored and remembered for his brave actions.

The Memorial

These days you can go to the Summerfield School and there stands a big marble memorial stone statue to Charles Bruce, founder of what is now Summerfield. It is also in honor of Jamie Gillis, Lee's bugle boy. The children who attend school there know all about him. A beautiful mural painted by the students portrays Bruce's Crossroads and that fateful day when Jamie Gillis gave his life for his country. His story is well loved by the community and the school's students. They talk about Jamie as if he were still there. The beautiful monument to Charles Bruce and Jamie Gillis is prominent in front of the Summerfield School. When you go visit it, sit on one of the nice benches there and let the history come to life in your imagination. You'll see written upon the monument "In memory to Jamie Gillis, the bugle boy who gave his life for his family and country."

I've kept that story of Jamie the bugler boy all these years and tell it often so that the memory of that brave young man and his good deeds will be forever known. Sometimes I find myself sitting on my own front porch on my own rocking chair at dusk. I let my mind wander and try to listen for a few soft and low notes drifting in from across the field.

Taken from inside Summerfield school, this mural was painted during Cynthia's tenure as the school's art specialist. Parent, Joi Chapman, and fifth grade students created the mural from the history of the town. The children and the town both greatly admire Jamie Gillis and keep his memory alive. The caption below the mural reads "One Revolution, Forever Free – 1781." *Photo by Cynthia.*

Details from the mural, one showing Jamie about to be shot by British troops.
Photo by Cynthia.

Lake Higgins. *Photo by Cynthia.*

Echoes from the Past

The Arrowhead Chipping Ground

Lake Higgins is on the northwest side of Greensboro and is part of the reservoir as well. Back when the drought came, the water level there changed a great deal. It got real low, but it's mostly back to where it should be now. Most of the time, however, Lake Higgins is a nice, refreshing, beautiful lake. Sometimes the neighbors are out and you can stop and talk to them.

Grace and Charlie Wall lived in the farmhouse right on Hamburg Mill Road. They were quite a pair of characters. They lived on that farm and worked the land for many years. Most folks called her Granny Wall. It didn't take any time at all for her and me to become friends. I would spend a lot of time sitting on her front porch in a rocking chair sipping on a cool drink while listening to her tell me all the old stories. I found them to be so interesting and fascinating and would just sit and listen to her talk for hours.

It was her husband, Charlie, who found the first arrowhead out there. As the story goes, it had rained the night before and Charlie went out to do some plowing. When he did, he noticed all these strange-looking bits of stones lying all about. He picked one up and turned it over in his fingers as he examined the odd little triangle-shaped stone. "Was it an arrowhead?" he wondered. This was a while ago and schools weren't yet teaching such enlightened subjects like multi-cultural history, so he did what he knew how to do — he started showing it around to his friends and asking them what they thought it was. Most folks believed it to be an arrowhead from olden times.

Charlie continued to find more arrowheads over the years. Why, Charlie himself had shoeboxes full up with the things. They were all different shapes and sizes and made of different types of stone. In fact, Granny Wall and Charlie's great niece Maryann and her husband, Danny, lived with their sons across Hamburg Mill Road in the house they built back in the 1980s. They found them on their property too. Not in as many shapes but there were some prehistoric tools as well. Danny has a stone that could have been used for grinding corn and a bigger stone that he suspects was probably used as a hatchet. It's so all very fascinating. Just imagine the history that happened for hundreds of years right in Summerfield. Historians have determined that the area was "a chipping ground," or a central place for making arrowheads, tools, and weapons. These were known to be located near creeks and lakes since water was, of course, necessary in the process.

Oh sure, there have been other folks in the area who found arrowheads too, but no one had as many in one single spot as Granny Wall and Charlie did, nor did they have the variety of shapes, sizes, and tools. That sweet old couple may no longer be with us, but the story goes on and on.

The late Charlie Wall's field on Hamburg Mill Road, Pleasant Ridge, North Carolina. *Photo by Cynthia.*

Learning About the Past

The Greensboro Historical Museum has great exhibits and displays of prehistoric Native American settlements and the "chipping ground" in the area. Another good place in the neighborhood to hear local stories is around the corner at Wilson's Store. It's a thriving gas and convenience store, but for many years it's been a country store where folks gather to sit and catch up on the neighborhood gossip and happenings.

Historians will tell you that long, long, long ago prehistoric Native American tribes in this area had what they called a chipping ground — a place where the arrowheads, spears, and tools were made for their people. The area was rich in the kind of rocks that were needed. The forests, creeks, and lakes made this a bountiful settling place. To this day, some of the local folks will till their gardens in the spring and find an arrowhead or a stone tool. Taking a walk in the beautiful woods that are still around may reveal an odd-shaped rock as well as echoes of the past.

Home Place

The old home place was a grand, two-story house with wide porches and huge trees in the front yard. The home place was of course painted

Photo by Cynthia.

white and the big spreading branches of the trees were like a beautiful canopy. Some of the trees were old enough to have perhaps been two hundred years old, and they were still growing.

No one's quite sure what happened, the family history has several versions, but it was thought that a big lightning storm came and a huge bolt of lightning hit and created the fire that caused the house to burn to the ground. Fortunately, nobody in the family was home or injured. The family moved across the street to the little white house that sat on the other side of the farm on Pleasant Ridge Road. The family carried on with life as usual. They soon settled in, enjoying the house.

By then, the family had opened a little country store at the crossroads right there at Carlson Dairy Road and what's now Pleasant Ridge Road. It became a busy place over the years. Still is. Yes, the little store is thriving. You can drive by now and see a row of fellas sitting outside in nice weather. They're telling old stories and keeping up with the neighborhood. The little white house is still there too. The family moved to a newer house down the road when the children were grown. To this day most of 'em continue to live nearby. The house was sold several times over the years. Of course the neighborhood has changed some too. New houses were built where the old home place was. Another one is next to Grace and Charlie Wall's old farm. Hamburg Mill Road and Pleasant Ridge Road have become busy roads instead of sleepy byways.

Since the old days, the home place has really changed. Why, different folks have owned it over the years and each time that one of them moved in, they would renovate it and change the house to suit their liking. They added some porches and paint with fancy colors. Oddly enough, most of the people who owned the house only stayed there for a few years before selling and moving on. Also, very strange, none of the owners had children. Dogs and kitty cats yes, but not children. John bought it in the 1990s. He planned to stay and so he has. He restored the home and improved upon it. A new porch with columns and he landscaped the front yard so beautifully. More recently, a sunroom was added onto the back of the home and it's now quite a grand little house from what it was in the beginning.

John is a modern guy who grew up down the road in Virginia. He is a computer expert with a good job, not someone you'd think of as "weird" or "strange." He really had a good feeling about the house, so he wasn't frightened when the events started happening. He wasn't a scared type of person; instead he was matter-of-fact about the strange things that go on in his home.

Odd noises and creaks weren't alarming in a house that old, but one afternoon John was asleep on the couch with Rupert, his German schnauzer. Rupert began a deep growl in the back of his throat. John was startled to hear a loud BANG! BANG! BANG! on the front door. He jumped up to answer it, flinging the door wide open. No one was there!

The front porch, the yard, and the street were all eerily empty. Shaken, John closed the heavy door and tried to calm down. What was that?

He stepped outside and closed the door quickly, frightened, and locked it tight behind him. Then he walked around the house to the backyard and looked around back there too, but the yard was empty.

Rupert the schnauzer was still in the front room just growling that low growl in his voice. John was so startled and frightened that he couldn't go to sleep for a long time that night. He tossed and turned in the bed thinking, "What was that?"

He told folks about it the next day and everybody said, 'Oh it was probably somebody playing a trick and drove on off before you could see them.' John, though, just had a feeling.

Strange things continued to happen. Some of the events were just a little bothersome, yet none were sinister or terribly frightening. Well, some were even funny. John's friend, Brian, came to visit one spring. They had a big fancy party the night before, so that afternoon Brian decided he was going to take a nap. The upstairs had been finished off real pretty with a guest bedroom and bath. Brian was in that guest room lying down and John was downstairs when he heard some rattling around. Then he heard some screaming and Brian came racing down the stairs saying, "OK, who was just up there poking me and waking me up after only a half hour nap?"

John said, "What are you talking about? You're up there alone!"

"Humph! You've got to be kidding," said Brian. "I know you were up there poking me, poking me in the arm. Why, I bet I got bruised where you were poking me so hard to wake me up."

John just shook his head. "I wasn't up there — nobody else is in the house." Then he got a feeling and a look. "Uhhhh, then who was it?"

It was a joke for a while. Brian would warn other friends visiting about the "ghost" who wouldn't let you nap.

When it happened again, Brian decided he was scared of the ghost and refused to go back upstairs alone. He slept on the couch that night with Rupert to keep watch.

The next time Brian came to visit, he slept in the guest room downstairs. This time when he went to nap at that same odd time in the afternoon, the ghost got him again. It happened just as he was about to lie down to sleep. He was getting ready to get into the bed. It was a nicely made bed with a crisp and tight bedspread. However, there on the pillow was as an imprint as if someone had just lain on that bed and might be lying there still.

Brian ran into the living room screaming and hollering. There were a few more folks around this time and of course they didn't believe him. He took them over to the room to show them but the bed was smooth.

It was as if someone had lain there and gotten up. You can imagine how strange that is. So, did the waking spirit ever visit anyone else? John's sister was awakened upstairs in later years. Most of the ghostly visits were in the afternoon, though.

Anything else? Well... One afternoon, John was in the bedroom and thought he saw a blur, a shadow. You know how it is when you see something out of the corner of your eye. Well, he thought he saw a shadow or a glimpse of something gray. He whirled around to see who it was. Then he saw something there what seemed to be a gray figure of a lady almost as gray as fog. She vanished in the blink of an eye. He started believing then that his little house, the home place, was ghostly haunted by a lady spirit. The house had a warm, good feeling. The lady spirit wasn't malevolent, just passive.

Soon the neighborhood folks were telling it. John didn't want to start telling it for fear people would think he was nutty, you know, modern society and all, but he happened to be down at the country store and he told it one day. Some folks remembered that the grandfather had suffered a heart attack in the front yard and died under the big magnolia tree.

That magnolia tree was still there when John moved in, but he just had the feeling it wasn't a grandpa haunting his house. He said, "I know this is a lady. I saw her shadow."

Well, one day as John sat in his rocking chair in the living room by the fire, Rupert was sleeping when it happened — that banging on the front door! He jumped up even faster this time and had a baseball bat ready because he was just ready for anything.

He tore open that door. By now he had one of those nice fancy storm glass doors so he could see right out and he turned that light on but nothing was there and the storm door was locked.

Nowadays some folks say they would like to come visit that little white house on Pleasant Ridge Road. If it is haunted, there's no need to worry — the ghosts are friendly.

The house must be rather welcoming as a lot of their friends like to come and visit, but... perhaps the spirit or spirits are sensitive around visitors. A few years ago, when John's dear mother passed away, he brought her urn home for just a day or two before they took it up on into the mountains of Virginia to lay her to rest with the family. One evening, friends sat in the living room. Someone glanced up and said, "John, you didn't tell us anybody else is here. Who is that lady?"

John looked up very quickly, but didn't see anyone. His friend said that he'd seen a lady go from the front bedroom to the back bedroom just quickly through the hall. Everyone jumped up to investigate, but both bedrooms were empty. The gray lady had vanished. Later, John in reflection decided that it was probably his mama looking out for him while she was there.

Nobody's seen the ghost since and John's mother is laid to rest now. It's a true story, but every now and then, John will hear those footsteps and get that feeling that he is not alone in the house.

Mike lives there now with John, but he hasn't seen or felt any visits from the spirits. They don't take as many naps or have as much company stay upstairs. There hasn't been anymore banging on the front door or anything more startling than that lately. Sadly, John and Mike had to chop down the magnolia tree. John didn't want to cut it down, but it had to be done as it was ill and could not be saved. After that it seemed like maybe Grandpa Ghost was resting in peace. With the magnolia gone, John and Mike planted another tree in its place, a beautiful flowering one.

And what about the gray spirit? Well, who knows when she'll visit next? If you're afraid, then you just have to be careful. If you spend the night, be ready, she might come to visit you.

Horse Pen Creek

This is a true story — I know it's true because I was there.

I had just finished college and had moved into my first home, a little log cabin. It had a yard filled with these beautiful trees. They were so huge and incredibly old that I felt sure that they were a hundred years old.

A cold, snowy day on Horsepen Creek Road. *Photo by Cynthia.*

Even back then, I was collecting folklore. I was talking to the lady who lived next door to me one day and she was telling tales of the area. She was the one who told me that the log cabin was over 130 years old.

"This whole area is very historic," she said as she began her tale. "You see, Horse Pen Creek used to run right up this ways. If you look for it, you can still see the original creek and that is where them British scoundrels ran away to after the Battle of Guilford County Courthouse. Horse Pen Creek is very old and very historic." She paused and looked my yard over. "Very old and very historic," she repeated. "Why, some people say that this tree right here could have been standing and bearing witness to it all as it happened."

She could have been right. The yard of the little log cabin home I was renting was filled with beautiful trees, but the one she was referring to was simply huge. It was big around and its branches were very large and flowed off the trunk, reaching out, looking mysterious and ghostly, like crooked fingers. The more you looked at it, the scarier it got.

Trees aside for a moment, because they were the only things that grew in that yard, I really did love that house. As soon as you walked in, you were just overwhelmed with this special feeling of welcomeness. It was not very modernly decorated but I didn't mind at all. I could not only see but also touch and feel the logs. The place had an old fireplace in it and a front porch just like homes did long, long ago. I loved the idea that I was living inside a piece of history. There were the occasional little things that happened when I lived in the home. The sort of little things that makes one think that a ghost is there, but never anything so noticeable as to be frightening.

One day, shortly after I had moved into the little log cabin home, I went exploring in the backyard and there I found a greenhouse. It was so old and broken down, but I could picture how it must have looked twenty-five or thirty years ago, back in a time when someone used it. I imagined it was filled with beautiful flowers and herbs and that further filled my head with other wonderful story possibilities. As I went on exploring around the outside of the little log cabin home, I noticed a door at the back that I had never seen before. It was one of those old spooky-looking types with a curved top. My little dog, Korkiey, had been with me that day so I decided that the two of us were going to go and see what that door was all about. I could tell by looking at the creepy thing that no one had opened it for a long time. I was in such a hurry to discover what secret that door kept that I didn't even bother to go and get a flashlight.

Much to my surprise, the door itself opened rather easily but even still it made that classic creaking door sound as it opened — "creeeeeak."

It opened up to a short flight of stairs that led down into an unlit room. My little dog Korkiey didn't want to go down the steps with me at first, but he eventually tagged along when he saw that I was going on ahead without him. I guess he felt like he had to protect me. There were only the three steps to descend, and they were old, so old. I could tell right away that they had been honed out of stone by hand — a flat grayish stone, well worn. The floor was made of packed dirt, not wood like I expected. This strange room must have at one time been a root cellar, and I say "strange" because aside from the flat gray stone steps and the packed dirt floor, the room was dark, damp, and empty. The walls were made with round river stones that must have been taken out of Horse Pen Creek when it still ran this way. This had to be the original foundation to the little log cabin above.

The root cellar was small but then again, over the years the log cabin had additions added on to it, and as small as the cellar was, it was still plenty big enough to give me a feeling of uneasiness, something dark and sinister. With all the imagining I had been doing earlier with the lovely greenhouse, my thoughts switched to this room. It was easy for me to decide to turn and leave right away, as I was now thinking that if I didn't, the door was going to suddenly close — POW! — and trap me down there just as it did in so many ghost stories I had read and heard. My poor little dog Korkiey! He must have been imagining that very thing too because no sooner had I made up my mind to leave the dark cellar than he turned, darted across the room, and zipped up those three steps maybe without even touching a single one of them. He waited anxiously for me to join him up there and outside, wagging his little tail as hard as he could. He was glad when we were both out of there, and so was I. I had decided that if I ever needed to go there ever again for any reason, I was going to be sure to take a flashlight with me.

Now, like I mentioned before, the log cabin itself had been added onto over the years. Its central room was such a nice cheerful and big space, filled with plants and sunlight. It made me really happy while I lived there. The bedroom was in the back of the house and having been newly out of college, my bed was on the floor just like it had been when I was at school. Korkiey and I used to sit there on that bed with both the window shades drawn up so we could see the nightfall. And then the stars rise.

Winter came, and it was one of the worst and coldest ones that Summerfield ever had. There had been several frosts and reports that snow was coming our way. I liked the snow so that idea suited me just fine. I thought it was great. The power was on; the weather hadn't knocked it out yet, so I turned on the floodlights. Korkiey and I sat on the bed like we often did, the shades pulled up, but this time we watched the snowflakes coming down. They were big and fluffy, drifting slowly to the earth. We snuggled up together and eventually we fell asleep.

Sometime in the middle of the night I woke up suddenly out of a dreamless sleep with a very strange feeling. Korkiey, who had also

A snow covered Pleasant Ridge Road. *Photo by Cynthia.*

awakened, was snuggled up right beside me and letting loose with a deep, long, low growl that came from somewhere in the back of his throat. I looked around, up to the window, and saw that the floodlights were out. I tried the lamp beside the bed but it too was out. The snow. The power must have gone out because of the snow. I started to get a little scared, the house was so old and I was there all alone with no lights or phone… and that's when it happened.

Sitting there on the side of the bed, I had just decided to get up and do something when I turned and looked and AGGGG! I screamed and jumped, which made little Korkiey bark and jump, because I had seen somebody or something looking into my room through the window, leaning with one hand pressed against the glass.

"Oh no," I thought to myself as all those stories you hear about on TV or see in the movies or read in books came rushing into my head. My imagination was just going wild with fearful thoughts. I knew, just knew I had to get out of the house, and fast. But wait…they or *it* was outside. Ahh, so I would have to silently go out the front door to get to my car.

The Great Escape

I went kind of slinking out on the floor, Korkiey in tow. I was wearing my nightgown and thinking to myself, "I have got to get something else on me and get out of this house." I didn't have any weapons but felt I needed one so I picked up a piece of firewood to defend myself in case I needed too. I crept over to my old coat, slipped it on, picked up Korkiey, and put him under it next to my body. I love my little dog but he was squirming and wiggling and making things that much harder for me as he tried to get on down and start barking, a trait that Cairn terriers are known for. As my dog writhed and fooled about, I came up with a quick plan. "If that thing is at the back of the house by the bedroom window, I can slip out the front door, get into my car, and leave before he even knows I'm gone." And without much else thinking about it, that's what I decided to do.

A quick glance at the clock on the wall told it was either 3 or 4 a.m.; I wasn't too sure which. It was dark and I couldn't see so well. Another quick glance was stolen but this time out of a window to see what it was like outdoors. The snow had fallen pretty deep and the tops of the little bushes surrounding the log cabin were covered, but it wasn't so deep that I didn't think I couldn't get out of my driveway.

Oh so very slowly I crept toward the front door, opening it as quietly as possible, stepping outside into the cold, and then closing the door back behind me, locking it, without making a single sound. It was so quiet outside, quiet as a grave. I noticed for the first time that it had stopped snowing and for just a moment I let myself enjoy the peacefulness of it all. Slow and steadily, not making any noise at all, I crept along to my car, opened the door just enough to get me and Korkiey inside, and then just as slowly pulled it closed until I heard the click of the door latch. It was the only noise that was made and I felt it echoed out into the night air, breaking the deathly silence.

It didn't matter anymore. Korkiey took that clicking lock as a cue and began barking and bouncing up and down inside the car. I thought to myself, "If I can just get out of here, everything will be OK." But my hands were trembling so badly that I couldn't hardly even get the right key in my fingers, let alone get it into the ignition. All my fumbling finally paid off. I knew better than to turn on my headlights as it would alert the intruder as to my location, but with all the snow I was as fearful of running into the ditch along my driveway as I was at who or whatever was at my bedroom window. The car started up on the first try. I slammed it into gear and began to back away helter-skelter from my little log cabin home.

As soon as I got my old Chevy off the drive and onto the road I popped the lights on, swallowing down hard on my fear, as I fully expected to be screaming, "Oh no, he's after me!" Surely, he or *it* would be standing there in front of my car. The headlights shone bright and lit up the road before me — no one and nothing stood in my way or blocked my path. I urged the Chevy out onto Horse Pen Creek Road and drove as fast as safety would allow, which all things being equal, was not so fast at all. I was slipping and sliding all over the road and it looked like I was going to spill over into a ditch after all. Nevertheless, even with the impending doom of wrecking the car, I still kept looking back over my shoulder to see if anybody or anything was chasing after me. The road was thankfully dark and empty, dark and empty as a grave.

Somehow and forever later, I made it over to New Garden Road and then over to Jefferson where my boyfriend, Fred, lived with his parents. I wish you could have seen the look on their faces when they saw me that early and snow-filled morning. His dad, Fred Sr., was more startled to learn that I was out driving in that mess more than anything else. They wrapped me up in a blanket and politely listened to me babble out my wild tale. I say that they "politely listened" because I knew that they didn't believe me. Addie Mae, Fred's mama, gave me some of her delicious cocoa and said to me in the sweetest voice, "You know what I think? I bet that you had a nightmare, a bad dream, that's all. How could anyone have been there at your window if there were no lights or without a flashlight? It had to be a bad dream."

I knew it wasn't a bad dream or a nightmare, as it hadn't felt like either. It all felt real to me and I knew that it had happened. Korkiey had been growling at something.

The next morning, after we all got a few more hours of sleep, the sun came up and was shining bright against the snow, making it sparkle. As pretty as it was, it did nothing to drive off the fear and concern that I had the night before. I wanted to call the police because I fully believed that at the very least somebody had broken into my home and robbed it. Fred's parents still weren't convinced, they still believed that nothing had really happened and didn't want to bother the sheriff over something like this. "Let's just go over there and see for ourselves," they said.

So that's what we did. The road had been scraped clean but as we pulled up into my long driveway, you could see the tire marks that I had made in the snow the night before. Every slip and slide I had made in my escape was still visible. Fred's dad parked the car and we all got out, each of us looking at the snow here and there for footprints as proof of the thing I claimed to have seen, but there weren't any.

Then we saw them.

One single set of footprints lay there in the snow. They went up the last step, across the patio, and stopped right in front of my bedroom window. I couldn't help it, I found myself hollering and jumping up and down. "Look! Look! Look at those footprints! I told ya! I told ya!"

Then another thing happened. Just as suddenly as we found the footprints, a realization came to all of us at the same time. We noticed that the footprints didn't go anywhere; they just stopped at my window.

We went to the front door. It was still locked. We went inside the little log cabin home and looked around. Nothing had been touched. Nothing had been moved. We went into my bedroom and looked at the window. To this day still, I remember what I saw as clearly as ever. There on the glass, before us all, was a large handprint etched into the frost on the window. Whoever or whatever was at my window that night had walked up to it from out of nowhere, left its handprint, and disappeared without making any tracks when it left. Who was it? What was it? We'll never know. As old as it was, I had always thought that the house was a little haunted and every once in a while a little thing or something would happen strange, but that was the most haunted night I had ever experienced.

These days Horse Pen Creek Road is really busy with traffic. There are townhouses and condos and schools lining the road on either side. The saddest thing was that one day as I drove down Horse Pen Creek, I saw that some developers had cleared the lot with the little log cabin on it and chopped down all those beautiful old trees, the trees that probably witnessed the Battle of Guilford County Courthouse. I began to cry. At the next stoplight I made a U-turn and went back to my old home. Driving up the long driveway brought back memories of the night Korkiey and I zigzagged our way through the snow, escaping whatever it was that stood at my bedroom window. I was overwhelmed with all the memories I had while I lived in that little house, both the good times and the bad. I parked the car and walked up to the path to my old home. The front door was open, as if it was expecting me, welcoming me inside one last time. I took its offer and entered on in. The place was completely empty, debris was on the floor, and some of the windows were broken. I could tell that it wouldn't be long until the house was taken from us, swept away to make room for something else. I went to each room in turn, trying to see if I could feel anything, but all the life and energy was now long gone.

About two weeks later, the house was no more. Later still some condos were built over the spot. All that remains of the area is one lone tree that somehow managed to not get chopped down. Every time I pass the spot, I remember that night in the middle of the snowstorm. The night the nightmare happened. The dead of night somebody or something was at my window on Horse Pen Creek Road.

Great Place to Live

Pleasant Ridge Road near Summerfield is kinda like living in the country. The only difference is the new, high-dollar housing developments and the twenty to thirty old neighborhoods, complete with nice houses that have acreage and woods. The fun part of it all is that you still get the occasional field of cows, corn, or big gardens. Yeah, I said fun. Who wouldn't laugh if they lived near, not across from so you have to look at him, but near the "GIANT PIG"? You can't see him unless you're looking or stop the car, but yes sir, there is the biggest

Photo by Cynthia.

pig you'll ever see lying in his hole. The goats and chickens seem to wander around him unaware, probably because he spends most days just snoozing and sunbathing.

Then there are the freedom-loving cows that are Giant Pig's family. Those cows just love to get out and wander around Pleasant Ridge Road and Hamburg Mill Road. One time, there was a big uproar 'cause of the two (or was it three?) bulls that escaped. They were eating the expensive trees and tearing up the nice landscaping in someone's "manicured" yard. Why, it was such an uproar that it drew a big crowd of three sheriff cars, two Highway Patrol officers, and about fifty amused (except for the yard owner) neighbors and passersby. The tale is still told around here because it was like a slapstick comedy. That is, until the farmer got there and ordered the "boys" back home. The bulls went on quietly. 'Course one other time the cows broke free and they were on Hamburg Mill Road. If you were lucky, you got to see a kind lady herding the cows off the road like an old time rodeo queen using her bright yellow Hummer vehicle. Everyone still laughs at that one. So it's no wonder there are so many tales around here.

Wisteria House

On a meandering country road in what is now Summerfield, there is a little house that sits back from the road. As you drive past, you get the impression that the little structure is sad and lonely as it sits there empty, unused, and unloved. You can barely see it now because twined all over the porch and the roof and spread out along the ground is lots and lots of wisteria. A hundred years ago it was the beautiful centerpiece for the farmland that surrounded it. Now, where crops used to grow is a forest of trees and there is little trace of the families that lived in the area, raising children and working the land.

Wisteria is beautiful when it blooms, but it seemed to have taken over this forgotten home. Here it seems almost sinister, as if it were trying to devour the house. But the wisteria is covering up more than an old building — it's hiding a secret as well.

The story goes that a few years back a young lady named Hannah saw the little house. She wasn't able to buy it, but she could rent it from the owner and decided to do so. She had thought that if the place was fixed up and made to be beautiful again that it would make for a wonderful place to open a tearoom restaurant. It was perfect — so sweet and charming, well, that is, if it were fixed up. Hannah knew it would be a lot of hard work to get the house back to its original splendor, but she was determined to make it happen.

The first order of business was to be the removal of all that excess wisteria. The plant that had most likely been a means of beautification years and years ago had long since gone wild. It had to be drastically cut back and then trimmed just to be able to open the front door. Then the next round of work began. After the outside was painted, the inside needed a lot of attention. The walls needed to be scraped and patched and then painted. The floors needed to be swept, scrubbed, and polished. It was a daunting task, but eventually Hannah was able to get the little house near to the condition and glory it once was back long ago when it was originally built. She had gone to great lengths to make charming little touches everywhere, including restoring the fireplaces. Period furniture made the rooms homey and inviting. Antique dresses, purses, and ladies hats decorated one of the front parlors. The soft sunlight filtered through lace curtains.

Although the house was mostly restored, there was always some work yet to be done. Hannah would often be in the house all day long and sometimes late into the night. She was never afraid or concerned about being there alone; she was, after all, in the town of Summerfield, a quiet and peaceful community. But things were about to change.

Late one night Hannah was busying herself by painting the baseboards in the parlor. She wanted them to be perfect and beautiful, as this was the room where the tea parties were going to be held. She intended there to be trunks of clothing in this room as well, and those trunks would be filled with costumes and period gowns for folks to dress up in if they so desired. She mused that maybe she would call her teahouse "Echoes From the Past," instead of "Wisteria House." Oh yes, what a lovely name.

Suddenly, she froze. Hannah had heard someone walking around upstairs. She so seldom used the second level since she didn't intend to use that part of the house for her tearoom. Mostly she just stored supplies up there. She had hoped that she was just hearing things, but there is no mistaking the sound of heavy footfalls being delivered by a mysterious stranger when they are happening right over your head. As calmly and quickly as she could, Hannah quietly packed up her brushes and left the house for the evening.

The next day she cautiously entered the little house, looking all around for signs of the person she had heard the night before. Everything seemed to be fine and in order until she entered into the parlor. Hannah stopped cold in her tracks because there before her on her freshly painted baseboards were handprints. She crept closer to inspect them, curious as to how it could have happened. She was pretty sure that when she had fled the house last night that the paint was mostly dry. She looked closely at the prints and compared them to her own. The prints were smaller than her hands, so small that she just knew they had to be from a child.

In shock and disbelief, Hannah left the house again in a hurry, but this time returned with some friends. She told them what had happened the night before and showed them the handprints on the floorboards, but they just waved her off, laughing. "Oh, it's just a shadow," they would tell her, "a trick of the light. Let's just repaint it." Some part of Hannah wanted them to be right, so when they offered to help her repaint the baseboards, she let them.

The following day, Hannah came to the little house to return to work, ready to do the next chore on her list. She peeked into the parlor and again there on the baseboards were those little handprints. She painted over them again, but when she returned the next day, the prints were back. She painted again, and again, and again. Finally, she just gave up and resigned herself to the fact that the handprints were there to stay. She decided to tell folks or anyone who asked, "Oh, we just have a friendly little ghost here."

Hannah continued on with her work of fixing up the house, but those little handprints were not the only strange thing that had happened to her there. For instance, if she were out on the front porch cutting back the wisteria or painting a post, she would suddenly hear the back door slam hard and loud. No matter how fast she would run through the house yelling "Who's there?", she was never able to see any sign of anyone.

As nighttime drew close and the shadows in the house became long, she would always be a little bit afraid if she were there alone. Eventually all of the unexplained events and the feelings of dread became too much for her. Hannah decided that she was not going to be alone in that house anymore, but was as determined as ever to get her tearoom up and running. She was sure to take someone with her every time she went to work on it.

Eventually, the house was finally the fresh and vibrant home place it once was. The beautiful curtains had been hung and accents of lace were all about. Everything was put in place and the trunks of clothing were all full. The tearoom was set to open and the folks of Summerfield were very excited to see it happen. They said it was like going back in time to an old-time home.

The Wisteria House was a quick success. Little girls wanted their birthday parties there, Valentine's Day brought lovers, and afternoon tea was popular with girlfriends wanting to gossip, but… It wasn't long before strange things began to happen again. Even while the patrons were enjoying their tea, odd occurrences began again.

One day, a very Southern and proper lady had come with her daughter and granddaughter to enjoy an afternoon's tea. As the three of them sat there, a crystal lamp behind the lady began to move. Her companions pointed it out and quickly the lady turned around. "What's happening!" she declared, frightened.

Hannah tried to explain to them that sometimes strange things like that occurred. As might be expected, the ladies picked up their bags and left, never to return for tea again.

It was upsetting for Hannah to see the ladies leave like that, but then again, many of her other customers seemed to like the idea of there maybe being a ghost in the old house. In fact, the reason many of them returned so often was in the hopes of catching a glimpse of a moving vase or a bouquet of flowers being moved from room to room.

Eventually Hannah became more accustomed to the presence of the ghost and was hardly scared anymore. In fact, the ghost was from time to time rather helpful. For instance, one evening Hannah decided to do all the prep work for the following day before she left for the evening. She put out her teapots and crystal and tea settings, making nice little arrangements on each table. However, when she returned the following morning, all the settings had been rearranged, and in a much nicer way. Hannah liked the new arrangement so much she forgot to be frightened and used that setting from then on.

Sadly, all good things must come to an end.

One day, Hannah was told that her little tearoom had to close. The owner was ready to sell the land and house; Hannah knew she didn't want a farm so there wasn't any use in fighting it. Hannah was forced to close the teahouse. Sad, she'd sit on the front porch in her rocking chair and listen to the sounds that the empty house made — the footsteps, the slamming back door, things moving about on their own from within. She'd do that very thing every day until her lease on the home ran out.

On the last day of her lease, Hannah said good-bye to the little tearoom, lingering in the parlor, looking at the little handprints in the paint. She just knew that the wisteria would return in full force and envelope the home.

She knew no one would ever want to live there with the place being as haunted as it was. And she was right, as time went by, no one ever moved in, the place became neglected again, and the wisteria went back to its task of covering up everything it possibly could.

So, if you're out driving down the meandering roads in Summerfield and see a little wisteria-covered house set back from the road, it's probably Hannah's former tearoom restaurant looking lonely and forlorn. You can't really go inside and look to see if the handprints are still there in the baseboards of the parlor room or listen for footsteps, as the house is somebody's private property, not to mention that the wisteria-covered doors would make it about impossible to do anyway. If you do get permission from the owner and can get the covered door open, whatever you do, don't go there at night alone, not unless you're ready for strange happenings to begin happening to you!

Rose Potpourri

There's a rumor that Wisteria Tea Room reopened in Stoneville, North Carolina. However, in Hannah's Wisteria House, she made her own potpourri — a wonderful smelling fragrant. Here's a recipe I used so that you too can enjoy the beautiful scent it creates. After you make it, reread "Wisteria House" and put yourself in Hannah's place.

Ingredients
† A glass container that seals—no plastic or metal
† 4 cups dried rose petals
† 1/2 cup dried lavender
† A small bottle of rose oil
† Any other dried blooms you want to add
† *Optional*: 1 tablespoon powdered orris root

Directions
1. Remove the petals of wilted rose blooms, and then spread them out on tissue paper or newspaper sheets to air-dry until they are crisp.
2. Put the dried blooms in a covered glass container and then add dried lavender, or any other dried flowers you want, and then sprinkle with rose oil.
3. Gently stir the mixture, add a few more drops of oil, and stir again.
4. Cover and let the flowers sit for three weeks to a month. Stir gently every week.
5. Now you have beautiful, fragrant potpourri to put in sachets, lace bags, or a pretty dish.

Some Colonial recipes call for powdered orris root as a setting agent. You can buy it at most craft stores.

Chapter Nine:

Topsail Island

According to popular lore and not historical fact, Topsail Island (pronounced Tops'l), a 26-mile-long barrier island off the North Carolina coast, got its name from the area's nefarious bygone pirate days of the 1700s. It is said that the pirates would lie-in-wait in the channels between the island and the mainland watching for merchant ships to sail by. Merchants, however, were wise to this trick and had look-outs keep a sharp eye out for the top sails of the pirate vessels, as that was usually the only part of the ship that could be seen from its hiding spot. It is also believed that the most famous pirate of them all, Blackbeard, hid his treasure there. The wreckage of Blackbeard's flagship, *Queen Anne's Revenge*, was discovered in the 1990s in the waters between Topsail and the coast of Beaufort, North Carolina. The Topsail Island Museum now features the history of pirates as well as the area.

Before World War Two, the only way on or off of Topsail was by boat, but during the war the U.S. Navy, in conjunction with John Hopkins University, took over the island in a project know as Operation Bumblebee, the beginnings of our country's space program. They built the drawbridge and roads. Fresh water was pumped onto the island as launching pads and storage facilities for rockets were built.

When the space program was dismantled in 1949, the government sold the island to the public; in 1969, Topsail Island was incorporated, promoting itself as a friendly, family-oriented, beach-living lifestyle. This way of living has continued to this day. It's also a quiet vacation destination with few neon lights and no high-rise hotels or gaudy tourist attractions to mar the landscape's natural beauty. The island now boasts of three towns: Surf City, North Topsail Beach, and Topsail Beach. There is a bridge that connects the north end of the island to the mainland. Only about 500 residents live there year-round, but during the tourist season, the population explodes up to 7,000.

Blackbeard

The coast of North Carolina is especially rich in stories of ghosts and hauntings and strange happenings. Its hundreds of years of history and all those possibilities add up. I was raised and grew up on the coast and was enthralled with all those mysteries. Topsail Island was our family's favorite beach. It was also the area popular two hundred and some odd years ago with that infamous pirate, Edward Teach, better known to most as the pirate, Blackbeard.

The island's history includes tales of the pirates and their ghosts that may still linger. Even by daylight, Topsail Island has many lonely and deserted areas. When darkness falls on the beach and the swampy wetlands, the empty dunes echo with strange sounds and fear-inspiring noises.

One evening in the 1950s, it was just about that way, with the moon shimmering on the ocean as the flames of our bonfire on the beach danced. We'd just finished dinner and my family was ready for some storytelling. The setting was perfect. My dad, Mac, was a U.S. Navy man, and those ghost stories that we loved, he knew them all by heart — ghost stories and many other tales of the high seas that we found so thrilling. Our favorite, of course, was Blackbeard.

The spirit of Blackbeard, the pirate, is said to have haunted the isle of Topsail for hundreds of years. On dark moonless nights the shadows on the beach and dunes seem to follow you. Perhaps it's true that Edward Teach does continue to guard his buried treasure. He was one of the fiercest pirates of the Carolinas. He was huge, over six feet tall. His famous swords were longer and sharper than anyone else's. He'd go into battle with his long black beard braided, and it would have ribbons woven into it, and it was adorned with lighted long matches. He was a terrifying sight to behold indeed.

He and his crew sailed the coast in his flagship, the *Queen Anne's Revenge*. They'd be looking for rich ships to go aboard and plunder.

Blackbeard liked to hide his small ship in the sounds behind Topsail Island, waiting and watching.

"Topsail, ho!" is what the lookout way up in the crow's nest atop the main mast would call out when he'd spot a likely ship to raid. That, in fact, is how Topsail Island came to get its name. Upon hearing the call, Captain Blackbeard would make his move. The *Queen Anne's Revenge* would sail quietly out the inlet to the open sea, then as soon as they got into range, they'd fire cannons across the bow of merchant ships — POW! And the unsuspecting merchant ships would be too surprised to escape. The first mate would yell out, "Hear too, we're coming aboard!" It was the only warning they would give, that boarding of the ship was imminent.

The captured vessel would have to lower their sails quickly or risk being sent to Davy Jones's locker. Then the pirates would swarm onboard their prize ship. Snatching all the gold, snatching all the silver, and kissing all the ladies.

That night, they'd have a big pirate party, you know, eating, drinking, dancing, telling stories, and singing sea songs.

"Yo, ho, up she rises,
Yo, ho, up she rises,
Yo, ho, up she rises early in the morning.

What shall we do with a mean old pirate?
What shall we do with the mean old pirates?
What shall we do with the mean old pirates early in the morning?

Photo by Cynthia.

Throw 'em in the long boat, Charlie
Throw 'em in the long boat, Charlie
Throw 'em in the long boat, Charlie, early in the morning.

Late that night, after a big celebration, all the pirates would be asleep except their captain. That's when Blackbeard would probably silently load a large share of the treasure in a chest down to his secret longboat. He'd row quietly ashore across the inky black water to Topsail Island. He'd dig deep in the sand with only the light of a lantern. Then, he'd bury that chest deep, above the high tide waterline where no one could find it. Without a word, he'd return to the ship, revealing the deed to no one.

The legends say that Blackbeard hid his treasure all along the islands and coast of North Carolina, South Carolina, Virginia, and some say even beyond. Well, where's the treasure now? No one knows for sure. The *Queen Anne's Revenge* sank in a terrible storm near the town of Beaufort, North Carolina. Blackbeard and his crew escaped and sailed off in another vessel to continue their pirate exploits, but... that's another story.

In more recent times, when hurricane Fran ravaged the North Carolina coast a couple of years ago, sands were shifted from a sandbar near Beaufort, North Carolina. Scientists had been scuba diving and they believed they discovered the wreck of the *Queen Anne's Revenge*. Yes, right there in only twenty feet of water, Blackbeard's flagship lay at rest. They've been bringing up some of the things from the wreck ever since and some of the fascinating secrets have already been brought to land for the first time in hundreds of years. Yet, they have found no gold. You can go and see for yourself down at one of the museums.

Where is Blackbeard's gold? No one knows, who can say for sure? Now some stories say he took the secret of the treasure to his watery grave. Others hint that he spent it all. He was quite a ladies' man, and had maybe up to a dozen wives. The most popular legend is that the treasure is still hidden, but beware — the ghost of Blackbeard is guarding the treasure to this day, according to legends.

For many, many years treasure hunters have searched, many have tried, but all have failed, and several have never returned. I myself have searched on Topsail Island but have never found even a single gold doubloon. If you should decide to go searching for the treasure beware, beware. Search during the day, as those ghost stories might be true.

Walking on the beach at night, the shadows seem to follow you and reach out for you. A salty gray sea mist rolls in from the jet-black sea, swirling around you, and the twisted gnarled oak trees and the live cypress rise like giant black skeletons against the sky. Out of nowhere a sudden breeze will move the sea oats with sighs and whispers, but no one is there. Odd lights appear and weave back and forth. Not like a modern flashlight, more like an old-time lantern coming closer and closer and closer.

Run... Run while you can!

Is it just your imagination that makes fear grip at your heart or are the legends true? Beware, and don't search those Topsail Beaches late at night when the moon is dark and the sea breezes blow. Don't go. You may think you're alone, but then you'll get that feeling that someone is waiting and watching you from in those shadows.

Is it Blackbeard? It could be. It may be that he's been waiting and watching for someone like you.

"Yo, ho, up she rises,
Yo, ho, up she rises,
Yo, ho, up she rises early in the morning.

Although this magnificent vessel is *Old Iron Side* and not Blackbeard's *Queen Anne's Revenge* it is a good example of a sailing vessel under full sail. This image is from my personal collection, it was a gift given to me by my father, Mack Moore, some fifty years ago. *Photo by Cynthia.*

Some of Blackbeard's treasure has never been recovered. This chest is an antique from a real haunted house I lived in up in Rhode Island. *Photo by Cynthia.*

The Legend

My family spent many weekends at Topsail Island as I was growing up. Our favorite Saturday night fun was to go for a swim as the sun set. Afterward, we'd build a bonfire, cook dinner, and then settle in for storytelling. The setting was magical with the soft ocean breezes blowing, the sound of the breakers, and the light of the fire dancing. Our dad was a lifelong U.S. Navy man, so his tales by the fire were of the North Carolina pirates. Blackbeard and his crew came to life there in the shadows. This has always been my favorite story, so when I began telling stories professionally I of course told "Blackbeard." For fifty years or so the legend of Blackbeard and his gold has continued with our family. Though my father died in the 1970s, his stories still go on. It is fitting that my niece and nephew listen to Blackbeard now, knowing their grandfather through the stories. That's the incredible power of just one story. I had to include Blackbeard so you too could continue the tradition.

The Maritime Museum in Beaufort displays a good exhibit of a few artifacts brought up from the *Queen Anne's Revenge* wreck so far. Plans are underway for a whole new museum devoted to Blackbeard and the salvage from the wreck. It is eerie to stand and look at a pewter charger that may have been for Edward Teach's supper. The stories survive to tell the tale.

Afterword

"..The Rest of the Story"

Now you can begin to see why I've said all along that these aren't "just stories." I have for all these years continued to learn and experience new stories, but the old favorites are with me like family or old friends waiting to come to the "party." I told the story of "Nellie, Whistling in the Graveyard" recently to five hundred students at an elementary school as joyfully as I did the first time I told it back in 1976. It's not just a performance for me or for many of my dear, fellow folktellers. No, instead, to us, it is a sharing with the audience of the many or few who come to hear us. When I am "on stage" I feel their energy and have a connection to the listeners. I am humbled that they give me their time, their attention, their feelings. That euphoria can float me off the stage.

Sometimes, afterwards, when I meet, greet, and visit with listeners, I am still amazed at the powerful impact the stories can have on them. As an educator I have been thrilled repeatedly over my long career to encounter adults that were childhood listeners of "Ms. Cynthia" who remember me with vivid details I have long forgotten. There was a college graduate I met recently who was a Head Start student twenty-five years ago who told me that she still likes my version of "Little Red Riding Hood" with the vegetarian wolf best. How about my ten-year-old art

One of the many intricately carved soapstone headstones in Pilgrim Church cemetery. *Photo by Fred Brown.*

student back in 1987 from the Gibsonville School, who remembers my ghost stories from art class? She recently saw me telling ghost stories on a television show I appeared on, so she wrote to me. She wanted to tell me how much the stories meant to her then, back when she was a child, and that she was so glad that I had continued to be a folkteller sharing my stories. That's the power of stories. They transcend time.

Folktales are the continuous thread through the centuries of civilization. Hence the vital importance of storytellers in the past and present.

Professional storytellers today are not actors who act in a play, nor readers who read aloud books — no, folktales are stories told from memory, told from the heart. More listeners and tellers have continued the new/old oral tradition over the years for fun or a career. However...a whole new vocation, that of the PROFESSIONAL STORYTELLER, began along about in the late 1960s, early '70s. You know, where someone gets paid to tell stories and folktales to an audience formally or informally, to two or three or even one thousand listeners in attendance. Unfortunately for us, it's not the salaries of millions that athletes or movie stars command. Still, it's professional. Most storytellers will tell you, though, that it is an avocation, not just a vocation. Storytelling is a "calling." Storytelling is very personal. There are quite a few storytellers making their living traveling and performing both nation- and worldwide. Folktales and their tellers are even more popular and widespread today than ever before.

All over the United States there are big, small, expensive, or on-a-shoestring gatherings called Storytelling Festivals happening. Many of the top professional tellers are from North Carolina. Why? I share the belief in the theory that our state is extra rich in folktales and the tradition of telling them. You can go all the way to Alaska or California and hear North Carolina mountain tales or a good ghost story from the coast being told.

My Network

Today there are strong networking structures all over America for professional tellers and performers. Here in North Carolina we have the North Carolina Storytelling Guild. Terry Rollins, Dianne Hackworth, Ron Jones, and I began organizing the Guild in North Carolina back in the late 1990s. Terry had begun the valuable *Journal of Tar Heel Tales*, which then became the Guild's quarterly journal. With over 150 members, the Guild continues to strongly connect storytellers and story listeners alike across North Carolina. For many of us it is an important support group or extended family. Storytellers are passionate about telling stories. They all agree with my mantra: "Stories are from the heart." Like I said earlier, it's more than a performance — it's an exchange of energy between us and our listeners. I still feel the "rush," as well as the preliminary attack of nervousness, as vibrantly as I did that first time I told a story.

During a recent Guild Winter Retreat, the members and I sat down to share some of our thoughts at a recent Guild Winter Retreat. The Oral tradition is so important. It can help people construct their own lives with stories and empower them to build on the past.

Ray Mendenhall

Ray was called to be a minister like Don Davis, Bill Lepp, and others. Ray and his wife, Ann, feel deeply about storytelling. Says Ray, "I found my voice and feel more authentic, more myself performing stories."

Robin Beckman and Mima Dixon

These ladies agree that they are book lovers. Mima cutely admits to having a "bad thing" or a "weakness" for books. "Kinda like chocolate!" I said.

Robin Berkman

Newer to storytelling, Robin too feels there is a need to educate and perpetuate the art of stories. She shared with me that "some of us will get the comment 'Oh… you're gonna read us a book?' I explain to them that the story is in my head and heart, not a book."

Sherry Lovette and Dr. Charlotte Hamlin

Sherry feels that children can learn so much from stories while Charlotte believes that encouraging the young to begin telling stories is of primary importance. She devotes many hours to training "Youth Storytellers" in the Greensboro area.

Charlotte's other great love has been the Storyfest that is a wonderful festival of tellers that takes place each May in downtown Greensboro. I've worked with her and her team to see firsthand the remarkable power of the stories across generations.

Terry Rollins

"I feel strongly that I am a modern-day bard. I am personally fortunate to be able to continue the ancient tradition of folktales. They are our link to the past and our ancestors. They bind us and tie us together while being a bridge between the past and the present. Especially as Southerners and North Carolinians we have told folktales for centuries. I was raised in a Southern family of storytellers and have continued on with that tradition."

When Terry and I met at a Swansboro, North Carolina, festival many years ago, we had an instant rapport. It's amazing how two storytellers can immediately "click" or have so much in common with a stranger. When some of us have been apart from one another, even for many months at a time, we can just pick up the thread of our thoughts out loud as if we just finished speaking together a moment before. Part of this is, we think, in the same "language."

As with many folktellers, we see life, people, and events in visual images. I feel this is a gift. This is one common trait most storytellers share, the ability of "seeing the story action in your mind." If a person doesn't "see," they must learn to do so to make their stories come to life in their listeners' imaginations.

Sylvia Payne

The editor of the *Guild Journal*, Sylvia expresses her love of books and stories: "For me, storytelling is a part of who I am. Even the stories I learned many, many years ago reside in me. They continue to speak to me as I discover new ones. They are all a part of me, calling me to let them out, to share them with others. Storytelling comes from my heart and soul. I often leave the venue 'stage' feeling that I have received more from the audience than they have from me."

Kelly Swanson

A writer, Kelly began performing her original writings. She approaches the art from a different path. Kelly has built her career as a popular motivational speaker and a businessperson. Her books and CDs are her very own original stories written in a traditional folktale style. Says Kelly, "Stories unite us in our diverse civilization. We can understand each other on a common level. Storytelling is a valuable motivational tool for business. With stories we are giving, not pulling ideas and emotions, we are giving. Stories involve the listener, because they can identify. It's not just information that sells but rather their perceptions via the story. Fun and interesting presentations engage any audience."

Trish Dunser

Another past president of the North Carolina Storytelling Guild, Trish enjoys sharing the folktales of her Irish heritage. After her husband passed away, Trish found friends and comfort in the Guild after she moved to our state.

††††††

We all agree that in this age of high technology and depersonalization, storytelling is even more essential now and in our future. The history, the past, the thread that knits us together to the present, is folktales. So folktales will continue for generations to come — told by folks to other folks and thereby keeping the stories alive.

Bibliography and Resources

Brown, Cynthia Moore. "Stories from the Graveyard, audio CD." Greensboro, North Carolina: Sound Lab, 2006.

Feintuch, Burt. *The Conversation of Culture: Folklorists and the Public Sector.* Lexington, Kentucky: The University Press of Kentucky, 1988.

Harden, John. *Tar Heel Ghosts.* Chapel Hill, North Carolina: University of North Carolina Press, 1954.

Neese, Everet J. *Dutch Settlement at Abbotts Creek: A History of Pilgrim Reformed United Church of Christ, Lexington, North Carolina, Ca. 1753 to 1979.* Winston-Salem, North Carolina: Hunter Publishing Company, 1979.

North Carolina Storyteller's Guild – http://www.ncstoryguild.org/

Parce, Mead. *Twice-Told True Tales of the Blue Ridge and Great Smokies.* Hendersonville, North Carolina: Harmon Den Press, Inc, 1995.

Reynolds, James. *Ghosts in American Houses.* New York, New York: Bonanza Books, 1955.

Russell, Randy and Janet Barnett. *Mountain Ghost Stories and Curious Tales of Western North Carolina.* Winston-Salem, North Carolina: John F. Blair, 1988.

Sims, Martha C and Martin Stephens. *Living Folklore: An Introduction to the Study of People and their Traditions.* Logan, Ohio: Ohio State University Press, 2005.

Index